THE 49 STEPS
TO A BRIGHT LIFE

A Conspiracy for Personal Success

PHIL MURRAY

First published by

PeRFECT WORDS and MUSIC Limited

1996

Copyright © 1996 Phil Murray

British Library Cataloguing-in-Publication Data available

ISBN 1-898716-85-4

Printed in Great Britain by Elite Printing Services East Grinstead West Sussex this book is dedicated to

The Storyteller

who lives within us all

Purbeck   Mill Lane   Felbridge   Surrey RH19 2PE

4 FEBRUARY 1996

Dear Reader,

Without stripping away the mystery from what you are about to read, there are a few things you should know ... a bright life is one which is illuminated by your own story ... your own story is that uniqueness which is you, unadulterated by socialisation and external pressures ... a conspiracy is, in the context I use the word, *a breathing together;* hence the introduction of an idea that we can breathe together as a group for individual personal success.

I believe in words and their definitions being a valuable means with which to transmit concepts. I also know that misunderstanding or not understanding words can be quite damaging to the effective assimilation of data and any consequent knowledge. I therefore urge you to look up any words you do not fully understand in a good dictionary. A few words used in this book have either been made up by me for fun, or, stretching a definition to its limit, used poetically.

I hope you enjoy the spirit behind this work and I expect that it will change your outlook on life forever if it performs its stimulating function for you, *as it should.* The steps are perhaps not as you would imagine them to be ... this book is not a course in *how to this* or *how to that!* It is a book which follows on from my personal development trilogy which covered firstly the body, then the mind and ended with the spirit. This book is about the storyteller, and as you may gather I propose that *this* is the ultimate function of humanity ... for each of us to firstly discover, and then *tell through living,* that unique story which belongs to each individual.

May you find your story and live it happily ever after!

With Love and Great Expectations,

Phil Murray

The Storyboard

Some men see things as they are and say *Why?* I dream of things that never were and say *Why not?* ... George Bernard Shaw

The Apprentice Millionaire

One ship sails east and another sails west
With the self same winds that blow.
'Tis the set of the sails and not the gale
Which determines the way they go.

As the winds of the sea are the ways of fate
As we voyage along through life,
'Tis the act of the soul that determines the goal,
And not the calm or the strife.

One Step

One Night In Paris

My name is Joseph; Joseph Sondheim ... known to the world as Joe. Something happened to me a little while ago, which had such a profound effect on me, that I deemed it worthy of passing on, as an experience, to you. I am a teacher of Mathematics, and not one well versed in the art of expression ... anyway, no excuses ... this is what happened ...

One night in Paris, is like a year in any other place ... words from the pop song ran through my thoughts, as I contemplated that personal experience which had made such an indelible impact on all aspects of my life. The only cognition any of us need for a happy life had been presented to me. It wasn't clear how, and required much thought afterwards, but that self realisation was now mine forever.

It happened three months ago, whilst on a short break in France ...

To be there, or indeed anywhere else but home had been to say the least ... essential! If I was to be in France, then Paris would be inevitable for some part of the stay. So there I sat, in a booth of a typical corner café, much like thousands of others spread across the face of Paris. The sound of traffic and constant use of French car horns in anger, made brief forays across the face of my jumbled thoughts. The aroma of fresh coffee and Gitannes cigarettes helped glue the experience to my subconscious mind forever.

The French were about to recommence experiments with nuclear bombs in the South Pacific ... Mururoa Atoll to be precise. They were the only ones who thought this a good idea! The poor Tahitians were appalled at the idea, and also worried that if they became too vocal with their condemnations, France would punish them economically. The Australians didn't give a damn about diplomacy and openly threatened all in favour of that particular planetary crime with repercussions exaggerated out of all proportion. The French stated that their planned explosions would be harmless ... all environmental protagonists replied in simple logic that if this was so, why did France not allow the explosions to occur in France? My mathematical logic did not argue with this reasoning!

Anyway, no valid reply was forthcoming from any department of the French authorities! I donated twenty pounds to the cause, bought a Family membership with Greenpeace and travelled to France for a break, and Paris for the purpose of protest. I no longer had a Family, and it was only my habitual optimism which guided my hand to tick the box on the Greenpeace application form indicating that I spoke for them all. They had left me ... or had I left them? Whichever, the result was the same ... those close ties of trust and friendship built over a period of many years were cut, and replaced with ugly misgivings and suspicion. I was about to indulge for the umpteenth time in circuitry thought of blame, shame and perhaps regret, when my ears tuned in to a conversation from the booth immediately behind the one in which I sat.

I could not see the participants, but guessed that the female voice, which was full of understanding, belonged to some kind of therapist ... not a psychologist or psychiatrist ... but someone who had chanced beyond the mainstream teachings available in so many universities around the world. No, this voice was the vocal representation of an awareness I had not heard before, and yet I knew it to be truthful in its wisdom.

The other voice seemed scared!

An archetypical Frenchman wearing a beret and sitting within my field of vision, briefly disturbed my eavesdropping concentration. He drank an Espresso as if in punishment, lit a Galloise and threw the packet onto the table, apparently in temper, and perhaps in disgust at a passing thought. I wished he could hear the lady behind me, as I passively inhaled some of his stray smoke. The nicotine artificially stimulated my consciousness and I once again listened in without the slightest guilt.

Everywhere I look, together with each thought I allow, teaches me that life is not what I intended, said the patient.

There was a brief pause.

What did you intend? responded the magnetic voice of reason.

I was excited ... without referring specifically to the incidentals of my recent troubles, this chance overheard conversation seemed so relevant and positive.

I am strong and used to having things my own way, continued the patient.

Which way is that? asked the therapist.

The right way; I always consider others you know, and base my actions around what I consider to be right! I call this my pan determination ... across all viewpoints.

The therapist cleared her throat ... *and do the other viewpoints agree?*

Eventually!

I could tell that some kind of cognition, or self realisation had dawned on the patient as he delivered his ugly, *eventually,* conclusion.

What is your story my friend? Why are you here? Unfold your story and life will fall into place. Your Family will return and all the petty squabbles of a thousand lifetimes will float away on a cloud of understanding, inspired the therapist.

So this person had Family troubles? I was not alone. I had to interrupt ... but it would be so rude ... they would know I had been listening to not only a private conversation, but one which could also be deemed intimate. Should I ask if I can meet the female voice later? I wondered, and then sank deeply into split second thought. Two Englishmen sporting short haircuts sat at the counter, and antagonised the Frenchman smoking Galloise about the interdependent venture which had culminated in the only supersonic passenger aeroplane this world has ever known becoming a raging success. They had been on the same protest as me earlier that day, but thankfully I was not recognised ...

Concorde, they giggled, *the only thing you French made for it were the seat cushions!*

I then knew why his manner had been angry. The Frenchman was a lorry driver whose vehicle had been blocked in by protesters. This type of antagonism seemed like a microcosm of something so much bigger ... but the conversation ... I wanted more ...

Each of us begins this Earthly existence with a story to live, continued the therapist, *but few actually spend time to discover what that story really is. The human being is too busy living someone else's idea of their story to contact the real one. They become so fixated with other people's expectations of their lives, that the genuine soul story drifts further and further from their awareness, and eventually hides itself in a miasma of mental pollution.*

But I have broken my rule by speaking too much ... we have two ears and one mouth my friend ... I have used them disproportionately.

No, pleaded the patient, *please tell me more ... I have to know how to live my story. How?*

There was a silence.

I could no longer restrain my enthusiasm. *Is it too late to contact my story,* I asked, whilst turning to face the owners of those two voices I was understanding so well.

The therapist and patient had disappeared ... no one remained in that booth immediately behind me. The Cashier looked my way, and the angry Frenchman eyed me with suspicion. I paid my bill and walked over to the waiter ... *where have those two people gone who were sat talking just behind me,* I asked.

The Waiter stared blankly at me ... *nobody sat behind you monsieur; in fact there are no seats in that booth, they are being repaired.*

I know you, stated one of the antagonistic Englishmen.

I doubt it, I replied sarcastically, whilst running to the door, determined to find the owner of that magnetic voice, *I don't even know myself!*

It was dark outside ... the street lighting played tricks on my perceptions. I thought I saw the owners of those voices a few times that night, and even questioned a couple of holidaymakers returning to their hotel from the theatre. They were not guilty and I returned to my hotel for a disturbed sleep in an unusually uncomfortable bed.

I searched for those two voices all the following day before returning to that same café as night fell ... *one night in Paris, is like a year in any other place* ...

The realisation dawned slowly ... those voices had been mine! AFFIRMATION ... I KNOW WHO I AM

Two Steps

I ... Me ... Mine

The shelves in the mainstream bookstores are groaning beneath the weight of well meaning volumes telling all and sundry how to be successful at everything they do. These books talk at you with good intentioned stories of other people's success. Some are original, but most are copies. Some make you feel good, and many contribute to your guilt at not being as successful as they insinuate you should be.

After a particularly significant cognition about myself, I wrote the following lyrics for a song on my *Forever Again* album. My mode of expression is words and music so it was natural for me to do such a thing.

They were very definitely about me!

I've seen misty mornings clear into a bright and sunny day
I've been to Japan and seen the oriental way
I've watched the worst of enemies become the best of friends
I've listened to predictions saying that the world will end

I've wondered at the beauty of the mountain and the plain
Read philosophy that tells my I must be insane
Dreamt that I've had money but I woke up still flat broke
Lived in California eating burgers drinking Coke

You're the only wish I've ever had come true
You're the only wish I've ever had come true
Life is just a happy dream with you here by my side
You're the only wish I've ever had come true

Inspirational books tell me that I can get things done
They order me to stretch myself while I lie in the sun
Dreaming of the one thing that I really understand
My oasis in the desert my small piece of promised land

You're the only wish I've ever had come true
You're the only wish I've ever had come true
Life is just a happy dream with you here by my side
You're the only wish I've ever had come true

I don't mean to sound pretentious
But I feel I should explain
That I have everything I need
And you can have the same
Look into my eyes and let me hear these words from you
You're the only wish I've ever had come true

The *you* was the *real me!* The *I* was the *old me!* Read the lyrics over again and see what I mean.

Brimming with information, I was slowly realising that all of the answers to everything were within ... all that remained without was merely stimulation to help steer me to self realisation. The first personal development cognition I ever had was during research begun in 1976, yet it was a further seventeen years before I was able to settle all of my abundant information and awareness into a relevant context, thus enabling me to *be myself,* and also to empower my quest to disseminate this information for the good of all who cared to listen.

The cynic would argue that with the question to *who you really are* answered, the remainder of this book becomes irrelevant. Not so; just less relevant! Once the real self is discovered, a period of stabilisation, inspiration and orientation is required. It can be a shock to discover you are not really who you thought you were. I also know a few people who cognite on their identity, yet continue with old habits, too tired to change! I know many people who understand themselves and yet they still seem to go nowhere special with their lives. This is all part of the process. You cannot ever make value judgements on others. That is rule number one which you should be aware of in your two steps! Value judgements of others degrade the process of identity discovery for yourself.

A cannibal can discover himself too, without changing his eating habits! It is however, usual for self discovery to occur concurrently with a quantum leap in awareness. Such new found plateaux would be unlikely venues for cannibals to expound a philosophy still relevant only in the animal kingdom.

You are now waiting for me to explain just how it is possible to discover who you really are and thus begin the adventure we call *unfolding your own story.* You are perhaps hoping that the information will be startling, sensational and *one push of the button gives the quick fix.* If such is the case then understand that these thoughts are your expectations and not mine. I deal in forever, and pass, on the quick this lifetime only thrill.

You only discover yourself by spending time with yourself. I have called this exercise TTM, as an acronym for time to myself, in all of my three personal development books preceding this one, and see no reason to change this nomenclature now. You will perhaps realise that TTM is what Buddhists call meditation, but it is not exactly what many Christians would call prayer. I believe that successful prayer can be accomplished easier if it is preceded by effective meditation. You can almost see it in historical context ... Gautama Siddhartha Buddha appearing five hundred years before Christ, with his dispensation outlining self discovery and enlightenment through meditation. This harmonised with Christ's message of Man the Spirit capable of love and forgiveness, which followed, along with much instruction on prayer, and just who to pray to.

You do not need to be a Christian, a Buddhist, a Scientologist, an Anthroposophist or an Anythingelsist to practice TTM. This book is not about being a religion. To discover yourself, you only need to believe in yourself, and then set about the task ... you may like to try the following ...

Find an environment which is still, quiet and inspiring, where you will not be disturbed. Close your eyes and begin to get acquainted with yourself. Become observant inside your own head. What is going on inside that place which houses the most sophisticated computer ever made on Earth? Do your thoughts think you? What type of imagery is perceived by you? Do you hear, see, feel ... or do you have a combination of all three communication types available to you?

Do not get involved with anything in particular which you may become aware of during this first exercise. It is sufficient at this stage to become lightly aware of hidden potential lying within you, and hopefully you will get excited at the possibilities which you can imagine unfolding during your use of this book.

Your first TTM should last around five minutes.

If you have read my previous books, allow this information of which you are already cognisant, to reinforce TTM as a way of life, and practice the exercise anyway. TTM will repeatedly appear throughout *The 49 Steps,* as without it we would be unable to pinpoint the basic tenet of personal development which states that *you must know yourself before you can truly know anything else.*

AFFIRMATION ... I AM

Three Steps

It Must Be Love Love Love

The degree that you are able to love fellow travellers, your environment and the other kingdoms of nature, will be in direct proportion to the amount of love you have for yourself. It follows that once you know who you are, you must begin loving that person, whatever your expectations had been, maybe brought about through the socialisation process we are all subjected to. Voltaire observed in the first book of Zoroaster, that self esteem was described as a balloon filled with wind, from which great tempests surge when it is pricked.

Prick it! Prick it! I suggest.

Voltaire also recorded Zoroaster's great precept, in his story called Zadig ... *When thou eatest, givest also unto the dogs, even should they bite you.* There was much wisdom around in days of yore, even though at times it takes a bit of unravelling.

My research frequently takes me into the realms of Esotericism, where Love is widely considered to be the actuality which holds this whole universe in place. Kind of hard to believe for many people who blindly accept science as the only relevant tool available to us for deciphering the mysteries of both the future and the past. Mark my words as I write of my belief that science will, out of necessity, have more and more reason to delve into the esoteric mysteries which hitherto have only been of interest to various types of religion.

Bigotry and intolerance of the unseen and previously unknown, will fade into the past, as more evolved Beings take up the Human form in their own never ending quest for perfection, and leave behind them after their next incarnation, a new and bright awareness of many aspects of life believed to be cranky and unworkable, whilst so many people from the old schools were still around.

There is an unregulated movement gathering pace which seems to be generically known as *New Age*. We must remember that, as with any mass of people, no matter where they exist or for what purpose, this New Age movement has many differing types of human being in it for as wide a variety of reasons that exist in the *Old Age*. There is a tendency to treat New Age as synonymous with Spirituality, Trustworthiness, Fairness, Co-operation, Interdependence, Love and The Future. I certainly do not make this mistake and I advise you to adopt a similar outlook ... this approach will perhaps help avoid disappointment and consequent denial of benefits to be gained from any connection with it or the people who comprise it.

Love is a concept frequently referred to as a benefit resulting from the New Age, and I very much hope that sentiment is put into action. As an outflow, Love is the most powerful force in the Cosmos and will always be a senior power to hate, even though both qualities are the opposite ends of the exact same force! You do not achieve abilities connected with the use of Love by opening up or buying from a shop called some name designed to tickle the fancy of even the most hardy cynic. *Rainbows and Dolphins and Whales and Stars and Spirits of the World and Earth and Planet.* We have an imaginary name for our fictitious New Age Shop ... The *ECOTREE SEATHINGS NEARLY NATURAL LOVE NUISANCE SPIRIT BIO-CLOT company of ANGELS unlimited,* and we pride ourselves in being, *a biologically beware company of hope everyone buys our products because we've named them right.*

Cynical, I hear you think! *Observant,* I answer!

People now pride themselves in buying recycled paper products which are not *necessarily* any more ecologically friendly than fresh paper. It was obligatory to raise public awareness of the fact that we were and perhaps still are, in the process of destroying the lungs of the Planet. It was not obligatory for big business to jump on the bandwagon by doing whatever it took to get that ecologically friendly label on their products, even if it meant that *nothing in particular was done as a contribution to planetary wellbeing!*

Why do I write of these things in this third step?

Saying is not doing. Stamps on product are not good actions. Buying a few joss sticks and changing your name to *Moonchild* does not mean you have contributed any more to the New Age, or the future, than the average business executive called Fred, who keeps business rolling along, people in work and the economic balance of the vicinity healthy. Love is a pleasant sentiment, but its significance will perish unless it is constantly utilised as an outflow ... do you get my meaning?

Love is an action!

Altruism is a better expression for many reasons, the main one being that the word Love is now almost inextricably bound into sexual significance. However, repeating the words I ALTRU MYSELF as an affirmation wouldn't quite happen Language is a constant challenge when discussing the finer aspects of life and you may be amazed at just how important semantics are when dealing in nuance and subtle differences of conclusion. Be aware of this, as you begin to explore the possibilities within the significance of Love, in this growing world of personal development to which I find myself contributing. You can contribute simply by loving yourself more, in addition to your other activities.

People are all so aware of being responsible to others, responsible to the environment, responsible to the business, responsible to this, that and sometimes the other; but when considering loving themselves they often feel guilty of self indulgence. Wrong! That would be vanity, and that is not what I am discussing here.

Love is the nearest we get to a panacea and universal solvent in this physical universe. Let us begin using it as an active outflow. Whatever department of life you operate in ... give a little love to your surroundings and those around you, and following my rule of Gradual Graduation, elevate your outflow in both quantity and quality. It is a quick fix of magic with everlasting effect.

Before you can try this out to maximum benefit, you must begin by loving yourself.

You may wish to LIKE YOURSELF first, but as you get acquainted with the inner worlds during TTM, you will find that loving yourself is more relevant. During your next TTM, amongst whatever is happening inside your own personal universe, introduce a flow of Love to the proceedings. Remember that you must Love the negative and positive manifestations that are occurring in there.

AFFIRMATION ... I LOVE MYSELF

Four Steps
>   Money Makes The World Go Around

A chasm is emerging between money oriented society and spiritually leaning aspects of our mutual world. It is not between the *haves* and *have nots;* rather it exists as a barrier separating those understanding finance and others who shun the subject lest it cloud their spiritual vision of a future new world.

Let me tell you ... this is the new world in which we currently live, and it is full of challenging and exciting potential. If you want to travel the ascetic route of withdrawal and abstinence, then I have little to offer unless you are prepared to consider alternatives. Remember that money is *not* the root of all evil; the Bible states that *love of money is the root of all evil.* In keeping with the quote which heads Level One of this book, I prefer George Bernard Shaw's sentiment, which stated that *lack of money is the root of all evil.* Some may add cynically with tongue in cheek that *love of evil is the root of all money.*

Of course, nothing alone is solely the root of *all* evil, and money certainly *is* the root of much pleasure! I therefore advise you to get yourself some! Get loads of it. Spend it! Save it! Give it away ... and for your own and everyone else's sake ... DO NOT BE AFRAID OF IT!

You see, a true Apprentice Millionaire understands Money as an energy. It is merely a method of exchange. Money is a convenience which replaced swopping goods from person to person until eventually you rid yourself of commodities taken in exchange which you didn't really want, but had to take in order to pass on your merchandise. Money is much simpler, and of definite interest to those of us who study energy; and *The Occult* is exactly that ... the study of *hidden* energy ... you will realise that money is a most occult of ideas, and occult is not connected to black magic unless the knowledge of hidden energy is utilised to cause others harm!

Money potential needs to be explored much as we research why light is white, whilst containing the potential of all known colour ... why grass is green ... and how we are able to contemplate the fact that if there was a beginning to *all* existence what caused *that* beginning, and not be able to conclude a totally satisfactory answer! It is a *ring pass not* of contemplation, yet the act of pondering the question may shed light on many varied and useful topics. I answered the enigma for myself and called my second personal development book by the description of my conclusion ... BEFORE THE BEGINNING IS A THOUGHT ... *and the absolute purpose of that contemplation is creation.*

I use these words to power most of my affirmative action for all considerations of life. If you want money, think it first, then act accordingly. Of course, I hope you do not expect that I am writing this book as a financial instruction manual ... The Apprentice Millionaire whom I enlighten, will become a millionaire in all aspects of life ... not only loads of money, but oozings of charisma, stocks full of character, surroundings of good people, cases of cheer, trucks of knowledge and bodies of good health.

I do not teach business however.

There is an abundance of material available about business ... much erroneously under the guise of personal development; so much so that the vast majority of people attracted to personal development are disappointed if a new book is not full of clichés, stories of other people's success, tributes to Henry Ford, quotes from dead American Presidents and tricks to tell you what your opponents are thinking.

Neuro Linguistic Programming is now a well known and utilised science which I described and acknowledged in my first book, *You Can Always Get What You Want.* Its potential initially excited me, when I concluded that it had enormous possibilities, maybe enabling us all to *speak the same languages.* Briefly, and certainly not doing justice to NLP, it involves the utilisation of three types of communication we all use during our path through life. Visual, Auditory, and Kinaesthetic, which is to do with motion and feel.

Knowledge of how you react, and observation of others, will

inform us that we each use different communication modes to greater or lesser effect. Thus, you would not describe seeing when talking to an auditory oriented person, much as it would be ineffective to explain the feel of a material to someone who needs to see it. As I wrote in the mentioned book, you would quite happily learn German to engage in business with someone who only spoke that language; why not learn NLP. However, as I observed people interpreting the benefits of NLP knowledge, I soon concluded that few had any insight into the dangers of using it to *Always Get What You Want,* which *You* certainly *Can!*

Learning what was meant by the position of someone's eyes as they were being talked to was a favourite of many ... to discover what are the most effective things to say to them, usually for the purpose of making a sale, and frequently to sell them something unwanted. What has this to connect it with personal development? Nothing ... until that is, we are able to use such tools for altruistic and philanthropic pursuits ... and this is definitely not the case I concluded from my observations.

Anthony Robbins, a man whom many favour with the title of American Guru, and indeed, a person who has done much to initially educate many in the area of human potential, must have studied NLP, because he describes similar technology under his own brand name of *Neuro Associative Conditioning.* I frequently utilise acronyms, the PAC(K) being one I have encouraged to describe the organisation I run called the Positive Attitude Club. The NAC(K) would be the antithesis of this as an acronym for the Negative Attitude Club. These initials are unfortunate as they correspond with Neuro Associative Conditioning. One thing Robbins certainly is not, and that is ... negative. However, *I* use the acronym for his body of data to mean *Neuro Associate CLONING.* NAC and NLP frequently refer to the fact that if you want to do something, clone someone who does it well.

What this amounts to, is many people contacting personal

development for perhaps the only instance this lifetime, and leaving after realising that it teaches only that everyone should get to the top, be a millionaire, have a super marriage, smile, copy, clone and cavort with black magic.

I encourage the unfolding of your own unique story, as the principle achievement available in this challenging personal development field. As my friend Nico Thelman reminds me ... *this world is not made from atoms, it is built with stories.* You are the only person in this universe able to accomplish this task of discovering your story, and I am one of many who can shed some light on potential available to you once the initial cognitions about yourself have been realised. If at that time and not before, you wish to share in the use of some tricks of the trade similar to those already mentioned, but in addition many more most definitely unknown to the vast majority of personal development teachers, then so be it.

All personal development has as its source, The Great Mysteries of This World. Infrequently acknowledged, but there for all to see who look beyond the headlines. This is because most personal development teachers are in fact *business technique cultivators,* and as such are in fear of upsetting their employers by being too way out, new age, spiritual or unentertaining.

The most well known phrase in our industry was coined by Napoleon Hill in his book, Think and Grow Rich. *What the mind of man can conceive and believe, the mind of man can achieve,* he wrote. The world of personal development still applauds that phrase today; yet it is an occult maxim, and if described as such, would bar the door of all but the most progressive organisation, to all but the most cunning of teachers! Image is still of paramount importance, and as long as we need to woo business, we will not make too much progress unfolding the personal story.

Energy Follows Thought, wrote Alice A Bailey in one of her many books written in conjunction with the Tibetan Master, Djwhal Khul. This is knowledge taken from the Trans Himalayan Teachings of Ageless Wisdom, which in this case, says much the same thing as Napoleon Hill said, coincidentally around about the same time. Yet, if I were to offer my services to the fictitious company known as *British Conum and Leggit,* as a lecturer in the above topic of *Energy* utilising data from the Trans Himalayan Teachings, I would not make it past Reception, *and I do know that feeling believe you me!* You see, Esotericism, Mysticism and The Occult, acknowledge the existence of fairies, gnomes, ghosts, elementals, little people and wraiths ... can you imagine me standing in front of a body of Conum and Leggit executives explaining the rules of life energy according to the fairies? No, we therefore only take from the teachings what is acceptable and this is absurd; just as it is ludicrous for the Churches to so call modernise themselves because congregations are falling. They think it necessary to appeal to the lowest common denominators, and in so doing they are denying themselves that position of altitude which they would do better to retain for the times when the lowest common denominators feel a need for their services.

Bring on the pop bands and the groovy vicars ... *the church goes the way of man rather than the way of mankind following the path lit by the church.* The media gives people what they want and similarly think it a service! They like murder, give them police series ... they're hypochondriacs so give them Hospital Hour ... they're intrigued by devil worship, give them Dennis Wheatley ... do you get the picture? Where is the forward thinking in this scenario? There isn't any! It is low quality economic blasphemy and should be exposed as such. Unfortunately, as long as the multitudes buy the tabloids which exploit their ignorance with pleas like telling readers at a certain time of day, to stand facing a particular direction ... France ... stick a finger in the air and chant UP YOURS DELORS, what chance do we have of guiding people into the values of character, over this garbage personality type sensational crap!

Meanwhile, back at British Conum and Leggit, the Board still want to play it safe. They have an image to uphold, and the personal development teachers often play straight to that image with all of the technology available to them ... frequently NLP. Before you know it, British Conum and Leggit, are training the personal development teachers to train them back again. The tail wags the dog!

Not all of us need truckloads of money for the precise process we have decided upon for this lifetime of experience gathering. I offer you the opportunity to use money for what it is worth. Visualise yourself with cash, big bank accounts and surrounded with opulence if that is your desire ... it certainly is mine! If you need to work hard for your cash then do so ... don't feel a need to restrain yourself or save energy for some future irrelevancy. To continue the George Bernard Shaw theme, he personally believed ... *when I die I want to be thoroughly used up.* Give it all to everything you do, and do everything well ... according to your story! Always remember that money creates an *illusion* of power; you are not your money and it will get you nowhere fast on its own. The Apprentice Millionaire knows the value of flowing money ... outflow equals inflow. It is impossible to be a great giver, and also to be unsuccessful.

Let us not forget FUN.

Don't get too serious about this bombardment of data, anecdote, opinion, observation and fact. It has little to do with your story. I offer only stimulation ...

Storytellers emerge from time to time, and remind us of who we really are!

Who are you? What are you? Where are you? How are you? When are you?

... and to conclude this fourth step ...

How rich are you?

AFFIRMATION ... I AM WEALTHY

Five Steps

Crying In The Chapel

There is no religion higher than truth!

Madame Blavatsky reminded us of this tenet in many of her Theosophical writings towards the end of the nineteenth century. I suggest this maxim as *the* spiritually stimulating catchphrase for the Aquarian Age in which we now live. A contemporary *spirit jogger!*

The Christians might remind us that their church is the true one, whilst factions within it fight wars, and rejoice in the misguided sentiment that God is on their side and not the other. Buddhists may feel that their brand of Buddhism is superior to the Christians and the Zen philosophy. The Hindus can fight the Sikhs and live in the same country whilst so doing. The Proddy Dogs can argue with the Catty Cats until God manifests in all of her anthropomorphic glory and priests become nuns and the vicars become devils whilst dogs philosophise on the sentiment of tigers.

Base garbage! ALL OF IT!

Yet it is still the order of the day for many of us to hold onto our own set of small minded seldom thought out philosophies of separateness and God Glory; the odd time defeat is felt through imposition of a more logical set of beliefs by a stronger personality, we can run for home and cry in our particular chapel. Well, you can if you want ... but I don't want!

I seek the truth ... I sense the truth as the beginning of a new journey and I know that beginning is just around the corner because *Before The Beginning is a Thought* and I have had that thought. Yes, while others were arguing and fighting, bombing Jerusalem and insulting the Holy Grail ... I was thinking! Contemplating truth and the insignificance of lies. So much so that I enjoyed it and became re-enlightened with a mundane belief.

People Matter Most!

What people believe in matters far less than the people themselves! Let everyone believe in whatever they like and shout out in celebration at our freedom of choice. Go cry in someone else's chapel and get the other point of view ... it is frequently a refreshing change from your own. The Apprentice Millionaire must not become involved in dogmatic platitudes of irrational irrelevance. Take your five steps towards a bright life by swearing an oath of allegiance to people.

The path to all achievement is a conspiracy.

The whole of creation is based around respiration. We were Breathed out of a Breath that remained integral. Our inspiration is the taking in of Breath for the purpose of creating the Path home to The Breath after the gathering of experience. This Conspiracy for Personal Success is an exercise in Breathing together. This is the meaning of conspiracy ... a breathing together.

Whilst much spiritual work can be accomplished alone ... TTM is an essential exercise, and self realisation is *the* powerful tool ... it is a Breathing together that will propel you along more intricate and advanced parts of the well publicised journey on which we must all embark at some point in our existence.

What is the less poetic explanation?

Interdependence! The most overused and abused buzz word of

modern times; yct, I still use it. The potential for you personally, if you are willing to interdepend your abilities dreams and aspirations with another, is boundless. In ratio with this potential is the infrequency in which true interdependency can be seen working. Businesses use the word interdependence much as the phrase, *or else,* was used before the birth of Trade Unions.

I know that *The Body Shop* utilise interdependence of a type, with the trucking company they use for distribution of goods to their shops ... they call it *open accountancy.* Each is able to view the others accounts and discuss adjustments to charges, if profits demand. This is promising! It acknowledges the need for profit and synergy. It abolishes suspicion to a large degree, and invites co-operation.

We do not need business as an excuse to interdepend, and we should be realistic in our expectations when first dabbling with the concept. You need to understand dependence, before progress can evolve towards interdependence. If that trucking company *had* to have The Body Shop as a customer, then interdependence would lack the inter wouldn't it? If The Body Shop constantly reminded their truckers of *who can fire who,* and the cliché that there are plenty more trucking companies on the road ... well, we are back in the Old Age looking forward to the onset of Industrialisation.

Likewise in marriage; if the threat to leave always hangs in the air as each glitch is contemplated, interdependence has not been achieved. Interdependence assumes that a relationship will last for eternity, or at least until a particular short term target has been achieved ... dependency understands merely that you will stick with each other only until something better comes along, and it often does! A bright life cannot be dependent on anyone or anything, and a conspiracy is an acknowledgement of strengths contained within each of the constituent parts of any relationship.

The Gestalt within each of us is a recognition that the sum of all parts equals something in excess of logical addition. In other words, you cannot break down a whole relationship into its constituent parts without the loss of some mystical ingredient. I sum up this potential simply as 1+1=3. When you conspire with a like minded individual, you have the logical 1+1 on the face of it, but as the powers merge and create together, a new force is born which cannot be reduced to its constituent parts.

This force potential is a way of the future available in the now. You must work with others, and with this end in mind, I invite you to assemble a Supergroup of like minded individuals, in the spirit of co-operative endeavour and interpersonal success.

When I formed the PAC in 1993, it was in line with such thought; although the general PAC is a forward thinking discussion group, my own personal Supergroup is to be found within its framework. There is yet another group at work from within its ranks which no member need be aware of unless it becomes relevant to their specific process which they are living. You can form your own Supergroup and interdepend with mine ... you can form a PAC and interdepend with all existing PACs ... you can join a PAC ... you can be a part of someone else's Supergroup ... the combinations are endless and the potential is vast ... but do not think for one moment this exercise is a quickie because it is everything but!

I am going to close this fifth step with a simple statement of my belief in the fact that a bright life should not rely on institutional religions for soul food. The church of your heaven lies within you and I advise you to invest in it quite heavily and frequently. Please do not associate Crying in The Chapel with other spiritual matters which may be discussed as this volume progresses ... I write here only of an encouragement to disengage from bigotry and separateness in all spiritual matters and I am afraid that organised religion has been guilty of that throughout its existence. There is no church without people and no antagonism without opposing viewpoints. People matter most!

You are invited to believe in yourself, with a dedication to love and honour that unique story which is yours forever!

May we all learn from you!

AFFIRMATION ... I BELIEVE IN MYSELF

Six Steps

Second Hand Rose

There are more fakes and copies in this world than is comfortable. That statement also sums up my initial repugnance to NLP ... the mimic aspect. It is fine to imitate many things, but the trouble is that most do it blindly and *become* the copy. Look around for yourself and you will discover people *being* their cars, *existing* as their job, *living* their houses and hoping to *become* someone else's expectations ...

I am cold so put your coat on ... you are hungry so I must eat!

You are an original, yet most of us look at others and see something in them more desirable to be than the identity which inherently belongs to us. Sadly this is visible more and more, but not solely, in juveniles who are subjected increasingly to unreal imagery of life from the television set. They watch lifestyles of flamboyance and abundance in soap operas set in the lush metaphors of an imaginary American haven, and next morning wake up to life on the dole in West Shields.

To some this is stimulation onward and upward to better things. They aspire to what they have seen, and ignore the story within. To others, they resent not having and begin a course of destruction during which the delicate balance of inner potential cannot be sensed as their attention is of such low quality.

There is no delineation existing to separate different types of people in this subject of originality. It is no more relevant for a film star than it is for the runner on the set of Batman 7. *Even Jake the plumber* can live his story, and don't ever make the mistake of believing that his story is any less important than the whys, wherefores and *importances of being Earnest,* Tom, Dick, Darlene, Marlene or Charlene!

The secret of being yourself is hidden in the subject of self esteem. This is where it becomes important to differentiate between the love for yourself already mentioned, and liking of that loved identity once discovered. If you are being a Second Hand Rose, using someone else's cast off ideas and dreams, it is impossible to like yourself. At the very best you can only ever like *them,* or your interpretation of whoever you have copied.

If you observe any group of people assembled for whatever reason, you will usually find a dominant personality. That is natural; but what is not natural or indeed healthy, is for followers to allow themselves to kind of drift into a weak imitation of their opinion leader. There is leadership and followership and no hierarchy must ever exist between two such camps ... you can't have one without the other ... unlike love and marriage! There is an art to following just as there is an art as a performer on stage to being invisible when attention should not be on a particular character. It does not make you a lesser person, or character.

I once noticed, in the Civil Service, a Clerical Officer who so much wanted his Executives Officer's position, that he began to speak like him, eat like him, walk like him and aspire like him. Good NLP, you may think. Bad DPS I would correct ... *D*elicate *P*ersonal *S*tory. When I spoke with this Second Hand Rose, it took an age to procure a reply, as his answer had to compute through the perceived viewpoint of his opinion leader. This was a bad case of Neuro Associative Cloning, and one which I was in no position to cure. Children often copy their parents, but this tendency should drift away as children develop their own stories. Some of us spend a lifetime cursing our parents for every defect found within and without ... if you have not forgiven your parents you have not left home.

Forgive and progress.

It is up to the individual. I am not proposing a dedication of reams to this subject. If you notice yourself doing what I called in my third book, Identity Substitution, stop it. You are the one who must be engaged in the work during these 49 steps to a bright life. We can conspire together for success, but at this particular point in our evolutionary history, one human cannot do it for another. We are here to gather experience and if another was to repair a fault in your make up then that would be the experience ... having the repair effected for you.

Begin to like what you have; there is no competition between what you have and what you want. Nobody can make you feel inferior without your consent! You are worth what you think you are worth and it will never be any other way.

You may perhaps know that you have a poor opinion of yourself, but what you should always remember is how little you deserve it! Create your future full of self esteem and vitality, whilst allowing the inner murmurs to surface ... listen to the voice within you and hear what it has to say ... is it a story ... is it your story ... is it a good story ... will you live that story?

During a ten minute TTM, get the idea of, YOU, and flow affection to yourself!

AFFIRMATION ... I LIKE MYSELF

Seven Steps

Last Tango In Paris

Never compromise with your inner story!

Do not doubt yourself for a minute and remember that you

34

cannot afford the punishment of a negative thought. Join the Positive Attitude Club, at the very least in spirit, and hopefully in every other way available to you also. After taking seven steps to a bright life, you should afford yourself the title of Apprentice Millionaire, but only if you are able to grasp the full potential available to millionaires, most of whom do not.

Having worked within the entertainment industry all of my life, I have come across many unhappy and superficially successful people who did not have a clue about true millionaireship. Many become addicted to acclaim without thinking to reinvest in their own true talents. Some get money which they cannot comfortably own, and try to blow it ... if they fail at this they occasionally blow themselves ... away!

Even after countless failures, which many personal development books teach you to believe as important steps themselves to real success, there is always reason to have that last dance .... the last tango may well be your success waiting to occur ... if you dance it somewhere you have always wished to be then who knows what may happen. If you dance it as a ballet to your own story, then the outcome can only ever be success, and this can only be measured by yourself.

Success is *not* fast cars, big houses and the executive toilet! Think it is and you may well end up flushed down the executive toilet along with all those stiff and old fashioned ideas that will have wished you there.

Success *is* fast cars, big houses and the executive toilet! Think it is and you may well end up living your story, which may somehow be contained within those trappings of success; but it would be a rare case for the possessions to actually be the story!

You see, I am not preaching ascetism, or trying to make anyone guilty for ownership of anything. I have many material aspirations which I watch manifest in their various guises as time goes by. I also, and most importantly, know that *I* am not *them.*

This mistake happens in the world of personal development when the public judge a teacher by the amount of students he has ... *the tail wagging the dog again* ... *the church following the people* ... what many do not know is just how many tickets are given away the night before a poorly subscribed to event takes place.

I know of a Scottish personal development lecturer who openly talks of the reason for abandoning his approach to teaching the public in favour of a designed programme for businesses ... he did it because the pay was much better .... and guaranteed. This is not living the story; it is saying that your story is not as good as the other one. The consequences are not always drastic either. The nuances of dissatisfaction may not be felt for years.

You have a choice, and I am not suggesting that you should disrupt your life right now and embark on a miracle crusade of inner discovery, to the detriment of all and sundry. That would be irresponsible of me and foolhardy of you. I have always believed in Gradual Graduation, and just as we increase the amount of TTM we engage in as more steps are walked, so must we adopt similar procedures for the installation of new mores and regimes into our lives, which *will* become brighter!

It may be that you were lucky enough to have discovered your story at an early age, only to dismiss it as unreal, before embarking on a career of someone else's expectations. I come across this scenario regularly in the world of music. I have friends who were brilliant self taught musicians at the age of sixteen. By eighteen they were old timers on the circuit, with an exciting future of big prospects ahead of them. Then they swallowed the socialisation process, along with everyone's considerations of responsibility, settling down, getting married, having a family, washing the car and loving their mums.

I invite everyone to a last tango in Paris; all you need is inner strength to break away gradually from any trap you may have unwittingly created for yourself, before stepping back into your true story. All you leave behind is a story which was not true. A lie! Do you want to live a lie? Do you want to die a lie?

Remember that trick of visualising your own funeral, not wishing for it you understand; but, for the purpose of self awareness, visualising it as a set of speeches. Have your spouse stand up and deliver a speech about you. Be frank; be honest; what would he or she really say about you? Listen to your parents speak their tributes. What will your children say?

Listen to the words and ask yourself if it is worth not being true to yourself. Have you ever listened to old people talk. They sometimes say things like ... *if only I had ... I once had the chance to and I didn't take it ... I wish I had tried!*

Do it while you can!

Phil Collins was refused a record contract for a solo project he was contemplating. He was in the world's number one band, but could not be visualised by others as a solo success. He felt strongly about it to the point of determination. He recorded the song himself and stored the stock of records in his garage ... the rest is pop history. *You Can't Hurry Love* got to number one and he has been one of the industry's top solo performers ever since.

Can you imagine if he had agreed with the record company executives ... *okay gents, you know best ... I'll stick to drumming ... I'll stay singing with Genesis only ... sorry for suggesting it.* He put his words into action and subsequently lives his story! Of course, for all we know, on his deathbed he may wish that he had been a round the world sailor, but I know that you will get my meaning. The story is inspirational for sure.

An artist friend of mine was offered a deal for some of her work to be transferred to posters for the mass market All that was asked of her by the company was that in order to introduce her work into their retail chain, she change a few aspects of her presentations. *That is not what I have in mind,* she replied, and promptly withdrew her offer. An unusual circumstance for that particular chain to find themselves in for this day and age of abundant art and not enough buyers.

It was not part of her story. She was also fortunate enough to have lots of money ... which brings me to the important issue all Apprentice Millionaires must know in order to keep them inspired. Having loads of money allows you to say no, much more easily than refusing an offer which your survival was counting on.

Get yourself truckloads of money and learn how to handle it. Understand the power which this money energy makes available to you. Lack of money can lead to much stress. Love of money can kill you. Understanding money brightens life. Having money opens up a spectrum of possibilities. I know what my choice is ...

AFFIRMATION ... I AM A MILLIONAIRE

Reflection ...

In this world of microcosmic mimicry, it is well worth being cognisant of the fact that up to year seven of a human life, the fragile entity we know as an infant, is still partially protected in the great cosmic womb. This is necessary in view of the fact that the Etheric Body, which will be responsible for the physical body's abilities to utilise energy without dependence, is still being built. Once constructed, it is an exact likeness of what one may view in physical actuality; it is widely reported by many researchers in the field of spirituality and energy, that this Etheric World, or what I have called The Ether Waves, will be the fourth dimension.

You will therefore be able to see a person's Etheric Body with the naked eye, and as we progress, this will be the principle humanity shall relate to. The physical body will evolve out of existence as we travel the path which leads onward and ever upward. Just how long this will take is an individual calculation. Many people already talk about auras; being able to see, sense and even touch them. They are frequently attributed with colour and often described in terms of quality. This is the Etheric Body.

Having lots of money is a visualisation process, much as is being happy. You are now in possession of your Etheric Body, having taken the corresponding first seven steps to a bright life; an apprentice millionaire must succeed with a balance of all that life has to offer. *The Richest Man in Babylon* is a well publicised George Classon book, written many years ago and well worth reading if you can enjoy metaphorical representations of what is in actual fact the truth.

It is written in a Biblical style; in our quest to unfold your story, I recommend this book of someone else's stories ... for stories are what this world is made from!

AFFIRMATIONS

I KNOW WHO I AM ... I AM ... I LOVE MYSELF ... I AM WEALTHY ... I BELIEVE IN MYSELF ... I LIKE MYSELF ... I AM A MILLIONAIRE

Men are anxious to improve their circumstances, but are unwilling to improve themselves; they therefore remain bound ... *James Allen*

The Modern Alchemist

Do not regret what went before,
The now is what you are looking for.
The now exists and forever will be,
In now exists eternity.
Your future happens in the now,
So embrace yourself with this small vow:
In whatever I do and whatever I say,
I live my life giving more each day.
My thoughts are good from my own mindstore,
Now is the present I've been looking for!

Phil Murray

Eight Steps

Spoof Spruce And The Spaceboys

The last time I tried to communicate with your awareness wavelength was at the very beginning of that time span you people call the early nineteen seventies. For some reason entirely connected with geographical reincarnation habit, the only area to respond was a conurbation in the North East of England.

I talk of response, but those sensing my thoughts were in fact unaware that they were so doing. They merely acted on an impulse attributed to originating from elsewhere. It took many tons of meditations to impinge my will on your Planet, and it was therefore deeply meaningful to discover that the sole result of my reflection was an inspired pop group calling themselves by the name of my cosmic Family.

The tone of my thought was perhaps felt a little later, by a successful performer who created an alias called Ziggy Stardust. The killing of that hero coincided with my meditative conclusion ... this is my last effort at communicating with you people ... not out of malice or frustration; only because the Spaceboys understand that *a teacher only appears when the student is ready.*

We hope that you are ready ...

Suffice to say, that my name is Spoof Spruce. I am a Spaceboy, as are my Family Spaceboys ... I have travelled the Path a little longer than have they, and I am therefore afforded the task of leading them into the light. This is why we are known as the Cosmic Family, *Spoof Spruce* and The Spaceboys.

Perhaps of interest to yourselves, is the fact that we are all male, and in order to multiply we have no need to breed. We are able to create at will the precise type of body we need as a physical vehicle necessary for consciousness and the spiritual expression of a presently discarnate Spaceboy.

There are Spacegirls too, but none of us have ever met one. They form an evolutionary branch that we have no need to contact. We wish them well and know that during one distant day, we shall join them in that great entity we all know as *The One About Whom Naught May Be Said.* The sexing of both groups is irrelevant, being merely a reflection of our mutual historical roots.

I am Spoof Spruce, and it may inspire you to be acquainted with a part of my personal journey. I talk of that time when all was not calm, and most were *dis*-eased by a universal *dis*-quiet which ruthlessly swept evolution into the fourteenth phase of a life, of which I am afraid yours is but a distant likeness.

Many evolutionary rounds ago, I lived in the World of Ether; creation was quick and constructions were elastic. It was very easy to change even the densest of material and travel was accomplished in the time it took to think. As talent grew, life became quicker. As speed quickened, hearts became unrested. As hearts grew heavy, love shrank.

It had not always been that way!

I spoke to the Lippika Lords of Karma. That in itself was an unprecedented privilege. I thought and they appeared ... that great spiritual group of service exists far beyond comprehension, yet they were there to guide me into a quest which would not only radically change Spoof Spruce; it would form the fundamental axiom which would be utilised to guide ten thousand trillion incarnations of Spaceboys.

I sought a solution to the unrest; The Lippika Lords were unable to help me directly as it is forbidden to interfere with the free choice humanity of which we are part, and which we must retain forever. It is through this inherent right, that experience may be gathered for the ultimate consumption of us all ... That Great Cosmic Family of The One Life.

I was inspired to seek my purpose ... *we all have a story which we bring with us into this life,* was the constant affirmation which passed through my awareness. Although my Etheric World was considered advanced, there was a tendency to drift with The Ether Waves into crystallised agreements which had been formulated, not always sensibly, throughout history, and as far back as the parallel universe to yourselves, which we inhabited many revolutions previous to your now.

The seed was planted into my brain, and this was all that could be allowed.

I was grateful.

I meditated and tuned to all passing waves of thought forms. The Lippika Lords were far beyond my wavelength and I now understand how sacrificial it was for them to degrade their comprehension down so many million degrees to a wave suitable for my aspiring awareness.

That they did however, and I saw hats. All shapes and sizes; the spectrum of colours and an assortment of sounds emanated from those hats, but hats are what they were, are, and forever and ever will be. Weighty meditations passed by as I pondered the significance of those hats, and it was quite by chance that, during my exploration of a particular hat, I tried it on my head. As that had been the obvious thing to do with a hat, I deliberately did not do it, for that is the way I am. It was an action which I engaged in unknowingly. I was guided to do it, so to speak.

My self determinism returned with the hat on my head, but it was not my life that I saw. With that hat on, I spied upon a difficult landscape which I did not like. It was not bad or wrong, I just did not like it. Many experiences occurred before I regained my ability to freely choose a more me line of action, but when that happened I grabbed the opportunity and threw the hat onto a whooshing cosmic stream of breath belonging to who knows who, and thankfully it disappeared.

The old Spoof returned and I thanked Galactic Galapagoes, but knew that something deep and meaningful was now there for the taking. The hats no longer appeared, but I felt an urge to find another and ask it questions. I took a deep breath of space and wished a distance, which passed; I thought of hats and one appeared. I asked it who it was and it replied that it was nobody ... it was a hat. I asked many hats and they all responded in similar fashion. The experience was wearing thin, as you say, and I grew uncustomarily impatient. I grabbed a hat and wore it. The experience was horrible. I grabbed another and grew excited with it, but it was not right. I snatched a hat which I recognised as belonging to a friend. That was fun, but I was snooping. The significance of the experience was alluding me.

I travelled and asked and asked and travelled. I questioned The Lippika Lords but there was no direct answer. *All I needed I knew,* was the habitual response. I sat on an island in a storm and looked. A number of other viewpoints sat here too; the numbers attracted an entertainer ... *The Modern Alchemist,* he called himself.

How can I discover what I sense, I asked, *I have tried on all of these hats and none of them fit me!*

What is your story my friend, replied The Modern Alchemist.

I do not know, I answered, *that is why I think of hats and they appear; I wish to find my hat.*

Then you must think of YOUR hat my friend, said The Modern Alchemist solemnly, *for until you do that, all hats will appear but YOURS!*

The cognition hit me hard. I left the gathering of viewpoints and pondered this new information. I then created a bright picture of my hat and it was the most beautiful possession I had ever beheld.

That is your story, I felt The Modern Alchemist think, *live it well and transmute all that does not harmonise with it, into all that does.*

As I wore the hat for the first time, my surname appeared, for it was written on the inside rim. The story was so significant that nothing in it troubled me. The story was me and I was that story. I pondered the wasted existences that had passed, but they were insignificant and I pondered no more, for the future lay ahead of me, bright as bright and purposeful as can be.

I am Spoof Spruce ... I always was and I always will be.

I send you love from the future and hope this personal rendition will inspire those ready to accept; for the relating of this experience is as much a part of my story as is the leading of my Cosmic Family, for in it, an invitation is extended for you to join me ... but not until your story is ready for you to do so.

AFFIRMATION ... WHATEVER I THINK I AM, I AM.

Nine Steps

Changes

Can you make changes? Can you change your circumstances by thought? Should you change something that works, for something which may or may not work better? Can you change your life? Is it right to change? Can you face the strain? Should you attempt to change others? *Can* you make changes? *Can you?*

Dharma is a Sanskrit word, which describes *the following of a PRE-scribed course of action, or one which is natural to an individual.* Other aspects of its definition would include, *essential and characteristic quality or peculiarity. Right religion, philosophy and science or knowledge,* would give an even bigger picture. This word introduces the idea of a personal story being present at birth for this lifetime, or perhaps at individualisation for those wishing to explore even further back into theosophical potential. A PRE-scribed story!

The religious aspect of this word allows us to consider the divinity within each of us, and also to ponder the connection between an individual and the great cosmic breath. At no point will I ever suggest *Fate* as an unfettered tool of destination, because I have studied too much antagonistic evidence to allow this line of thought. Also, you must realise that a story may never be realised if that is the wish of an individual, although I feel it unlikely that this would be relevant information for many.

Freedom of choice is that uniqueness which makes us responsible for our own destiny; it is this fact which strengthens my belief in the validity of the personal development world. This simplest of ideas, that we should all make the best of what we are. It is how we do this that frequently perturbs me.

We must always separate *the character,* or soul characteristics and aspirations, from *the personality,* or physical body, and brain *concrete thought* aspects of the duality in each human being. Big business has realised a tiny reflection of customer relations potential, and now many firms train staff in the art of smiling to shoppers. The staff mainly respond in a personality type fashion and this is what can be quite irritating when you are asking for a Beanburger in a Burgerbar.

You get bombarded with clichés and reeplés!

A trainee seldom makes the smile a possession instilled into their character. Instead it remains a *more than my jobs worth to not* type attribute. In the case of a smile, this is particularly annoying as that act should have a physiological reaction both mentally and physically on all of us. You see, when you smile, it makes you want to smile. Some message or other is sent down the lines, emanating from the facial muscles, and culminating in a memorandum to the brain which says I AM HAPPY; what an excellent affirmation that is too!

As long as the information is utilised for the personality only, this smile will only ever be a rather weak imitation of the real thing, which we can think of as the Buddha Smile, or the Soul Smile. Yet, it is a simple process to transmute a personality type trait into a more useful and longer lasting character mannerism.

The only thing that separates the two is a cognition.

A personal cognition, or self realisation, is the only occurrence that need happen for every step of the path to be an effective one, and equally important ... *a happy one!*

Powerful changes occur only when an individual realises some fundamental truth, and gets into action with the greater scope that particular cognition allows.

It is the cognition which yields glimpses of new horizons, and I am now firmly convinced that all personal development training must aim solely for self realisation, and not merely the inculcation of personality type habits into a modus operandi. Use inculcations only for the instillation of character type habits such as love, understanding and forgiveness.

I eagerly awaited a programme on television which had the same title as my third book *Empowerment!* Boy, was that an eye opener. An Under Manager ran around pouncing on unsuspecting, young employees shouting *how are you* at them. Frequently the response was truthful ... *coping; tired; looking forward to the pub; please don't shout; irritated by you!* When these type of replies were forthcoming the Under Manager would correct the employee by saying ... that is not the answer we give in this company now is it young sir or madame ... we always answer ... brilliant, fantastic, couldn't be better, *elevated, empowered, enlightened, cosmic, Godlike, Saintly, Spiritual and AT ONE WITH THE FIRM!* The italicised exaggerations are mine, stretching a point and using my poetic license.

I was nearly crying with laughter at the utter frustration of these young things running around *being how the firm say they should be.* The missing data was only slight, but small enough to render the whole exercise virtually useless. Affirmations, Inculcations, Mantrams and any instillation of desirable habits, only work when applied by an individual to an individual. You have to believe and have faith! We can also accept that a kid working in a Burgerbar is statistically not likely to remain with that firm for life; dedication to the purpose of that firm is probably only to be found in ratio to the degree the firm coincides with the story of that individual.

This could get complicated but I have my braking eye on that possibility. The fact that businesses are homing in on the potential of personal development is good ... much as *The Celestine Prophecy* is good if it encourages just one person to question life a little more than they did prior to reading it. We must place all data in context though, and always understand that the data is not the change. Information is not personal development ... all that surrounds you is but a stimulus to the cognition. It is self realisation that we must all aim for, and this type of approach acknowledges that cognitions can take all forms imaginable.

The Modern Alchemist says that change is usually a good thing ... take the good with the bad and place it in the pot ... transmute all that is available into a self realised cognition.

AFFIRMATION ... I CAN CHANGE MY CIRCUMSTANCES

Ten Steps
                        Every Breath You Take

Who is watching who?

Only you know when a fundamental change is occurring. The stimulus for self realisation can literally come from anywhere, and it is wise to be aware of this potential. Every breath you take has within it the life force from which you also originate. We are all a part of *The One Life*. This fact has now gained more mainstream acceptability. People like Dr Wayne Dyer have helped with this agreement, through being qualified as a Psychologist, and also writing about the possibility of *feeling the universe flowing through you,* and feeling *at one* with your surroundings. A kind of blend between mysticism and laboratory fact.

Cool!

We must all know a little about the *microcosm of the macrocosm* way of viewing life. For me personally, it is the answer to so many questions that existed, and I was thankful when my friend, who calls himself *A Silent Knight,* recommended a book written by *Three Initiates* called *The Kybalion.* I pass on this guidance to you, although it may be a difficult book to trace. You will find this small book if it is right for you however.

As above, so below; as below, so above.

This is *Hermetic Philosophy,* frequently attributed to an emanation from the mind of *Hermes Trismegistus,* and written many years ago. It seems in fact however, to be a body of knowledge written by many people and originally made available only to those who seek.

What does it mean?

There is a correspondence between all that exists, and everything is a smaller example of something larger ... physically, mentally, spiritually, or any combination thereof. We may therefore consider the possibility of each human being as a microcosm of the universe. The Sun being the physical and spiritual centre of our particular scheme with its planets revolving around it, giving life to all within its sphere of influence. The human being is the centre of a much smaller and less evolved world, with the liver, heart, lungs, brain, kidneys and eyes, all finding correspondence with some aspect of the macrocosm.

The purpose of this work is not to discuss in too much detail such philosophy, but it is as well that you know from where my research is centred. I also utilise the humourous way of looking at life ... when we observe the universe, even if God did not exist, it would be necessary to invent Him ... so that is what happened ... God created man in his own image and man returned the compliment.

49

How do these approaches help you get a better job? Only indirectly ... they help you become an improved human being and this in turn makes you a greater attribute to this planet, and plummeting downscale from those lofty heights, this could lead to you landing a better job ... figuratively speak.

The Modern Alchemist sees everything at his disposal as an asset. The potential in all is viewed as an opportunity for success. At one PAC Gathering not too long ago, a lady arrived whom we had never seen before. She sat all evening without uttering a sound, and it wasn't until we were all embroiled in a deep discussion around seeing problems as challenges that she spoke ... only one statement came from her lips, a well known one at that, but she said it at the appropriate time ... *I see all problems as opportunities!*

You could hear the cognitions falling into place in that room through her single contribution. We have not seen her since, but acknowledge her value as a member. It is an art, knowing what to say and when to say it. We can say that it is sheer creativity to manipulate another's inspiration and thus propel them onward and upward. This we all try to accomplish for and with each other. Acknowledge existence as *The One Life* and you may feel a surge of creativity within you.

Every breath you take is an opportunity. Every step you take along this path of 49 divisions, is a forever step to perpetual success ... I deal in truth, and real personal development is that which you retain after this lifetime has fulfilled the mission contained within its story.

How is your story developing?

AFFIRMATION ... I SEE ALL AS OPPORTUNITY

Eleven Steps
Walk On Gilded Splinters

At an esoteric study evening a little while ago, I found the attention of us all centering more and more on the subject of pain. Now this has always been an unpopular topic for me as I have had few cognitions in connection with this subject, except one major realisation which stated simply that I didn't like it.

A dear friend explained how he decided to forego medication when he had some kind of lymph infection in his leg. One good dose of antibiotics would have cleared up the problem, but he decided to explore the situation as an opportunity. He suffered in agony. A friend stood by him as his veins turned red and swollen. Three months passed before he was once again comfortable in his body. He explained how a transformation occurred for him, and this we knew to be so, as it was during that precise time period that he tuned his mission in life and made a significant alteration to his teaching outlook.

As I listened to a rendition of his situation, I suffered knee pain; I found irritability creep into my thoughts, as my attention became once again centred on this troublesome knee problem I suffered. Why was my knee *dis*-eased? I had spent a year researching and writing my third book called *Empowerment*. This invariably meant that I was sitting at a computer most of the time, or reading. The book was finished and the sun shone, as it was the beginning of Summer 1995. I decided that physical work was needed to balance my existence. I ordered twenty metres of block paving and spent two days kneeling whilst laying them. I have the ability to push my body beyond what is healthy, and it was on the second day that I decided to finish a four day job, *that day*. The sun was hot and I noticed the depletion of my normal body energy, as I began to push the physical vehicle with energy borrowed from the mental universe.

I achieved my goal and showered, before collapsing on the bed. After resting, as I stood up, my knees were so swollen that it was not possible to walk without severe pain. I remember cursing the pain, which is uncharacteristic for me, and demanding its disappearance. During the following two months, I conquered that pain four times, and four times it returned. I rarely use medical doctors, but doubt had by then crept into my meditations, and off I went to see my Doctor who promptly sent me for two x-rays, which showed acute irritation where a ligament entered my right knee muscle.

My whole approach to that opportunity had been one of domination and that dreadful cliché *no pain no gain.* Although I also utilised meditation, the flowing of love and certain colours to the cells in that troubled area, the minute my mind was elsewhere, a kind of resident irritation took over. The knee knew this and responded as would an employee who was always treated badly by a boss.

My turn came to speak and I related the fact that too much attention is given to healing and pain, whilst not enough attention is given to inspiration and pleasure. I believe this to be so. I was asked what benefits I had noticed through having this knee problem ... I was about to answer none, and it was at that moment that I realised ... *an increased understanding of others in pain!* My friends applauded and I cognited on the opportunity.

Patience is worth nurturing, and that particular sentiment is a constant challenge to me ... just prior to the story I have just related to you, I had another medical opportunity. I rarely have body problems, as I believe I am a healthy person with reasonably clean thoughts. I may sound as if I am quite sickly however, as I present two ill health stories back to back, but that is just coincidence.

I developed a large lump about one inch from my anus. I attempted to heal it during the first week of its life, but it was just developing towards its peak and seemed in no mood to disappear. I visited my poor National Health Doctor, who had the sad job of examining the area. That is mentioning little of what it was like for me bending over the couch showing all to my more than understanding lady doctor. She pronounced it a fistula, which was an abnormal and swollen narrow duct in my case, and promptly made an appointment for me to see the specialist for such phenomena. I viewed it as a crystallisation of energy which I had been utilising for writing the book mentioned in my previous story. Between the two of us, and with help from a strong course of antibiotics, I believed we could encourage it to leave.

Meanwhile the pain was excruciating, and it happened to peak during a talk I was pledged to attend. Of course I could not sit upright and this provoked some unusual glances during the meditation which concluded that particular evening. In bed later that night, it burst, and a greenish yellow liquid showed itself.

Around a month later, I eventually saw the specialist, who inserted a probe into the fistula and a finger ... *or was it an arm* ... into my anus. He looked at me with a smile and said that his finger was touching the end of the probe inside of me ... *it is definitely a fistula,* he concluded.

He described the surgery which would be necessary to heal it, but I had other ideas. I always believed that this body would never need surgery, and I remembered that commitment as he suggested the treatment. I had doubts however, and allowed my name to be placed on his waiting list. After two months I made around six enquiries and no one seemed acquainted with my case. I decided to cure the hole myself. By this time it had become embarrassing. You know what type of material is present in that rear area ... well some of this waste matter was finding its way down my friendly little fistula ... I need describe that no further.

The point is that as soon as I showed resolve and commitment to the cure, it *was* forthcoming. Whilst searching for *cure* tools, I remembered writing, in *Before the Beginning is a Thought,* about the most vital element a human body needs being Oxygen. I therefore gave this anal area of mine an external twice daily dose of oxygen using the hair dryer. *What are you doing,* asked my daughter one day, *drying his bum,* replied her brother on my behalf; *oxygenating my health challenge,* I corrected ... *Oh,* they both responded quite matter of factly.

A further two months passed before all signs were gone, but *I* cured the problem. It was a sheer coincidence that an appointment for surgery another two months after that, arrived on the morning I saw the doctor about my knee. Naturally I cancelled it and pondered that word *synchronicity,* which a friend of mine defines as *coincidence with meaning.* The strangest thing that happened in connection with this fistula, was that it reappeared immediately after I cancelled the hospital bed for which I had been, or had not been, waiting for around six months. I was warned that cancellation would mean returning to the bottom of the list ... *I can assure you the bed will not be necessary,* I guaranteed the nurse! I cured it once again.

So, it was natural for me to expect a healing for my knee after such success with my friendly fistula. It was patience that was lacking in the patient! I relate these stories to you in an effort to illustrate possibilities. There are many ways to view a single occurrence. We have the choice of viewpoint, but many of us have lost that ability to change course midstream.

Is your cup half full or half empty ... have you failed or nearly succeeded ... is every step one leap closer to your goal of a bright life ... can the good be seen in the worst pain? Remember an old saying from the world of Chinese medicine which states something like ... *One disease, long life; no disease, short life!* We can translate it to mean that those who know what is wrong with them can do something about it and live a long and useful life. Those who blindly consider themselves perfectly healthy however, when such is not the case, would fare differently.

I am not suggesting here that you do as my friend did and utilise pain for your next self realisation. I merely point you in the direction of possibility and inspiration. An awkward walk can be on fragments of broken glass, or gilded splinters of the finest diamond ever brought forth from this earth.

You have the choice!

During TTM, get acquainted with your body. Identify individual cells and acknowledge their existence as part of The One Life ... flow love to a particular group of cells comprising a specific part of your body. Introduce the idea of harmony to an area which has suffered stress.

AFFIRMATION ... I HAVE A HEALTHY BODY

Twelve Steps
Jigsaw Puzzle Blues

The pieces of most pictures are rarely in one place all of the time. Every picture tells a story, and most stories are a jigsaw puzzle which needs to be assembled with patience. Faith and determination are the two catalysts which are necessary ingredients for every plan preceding all success stories of which I am presently aware, and of which I can foresee in the future.

The subconscious mind is an inherent tool of good fortune which translates everything it perceives literally ... it can guide you to doom and gloom or raise you to the peaks of serenity. This depends on what and how it is told. You may notice that all of my suggested affirmations are in the present tense and read as if the sentiments contained in them already exist in you.

This is the way it works ... why I do not know ... but work that way it does. Similar to the physiological reaction a smile causes, tell yourself that you are a certain way and that is what the subconscious mind assumes to be the truth. Of course it is the truth!

WE ARE THE STORIES WE TELL!

When you are broke, if ever, and you affirm the fact that you are wealthy, this is true. Before the beginning is a thought! Everything created physically, was first constructed in the mental universe ... every single thing ... it can never be any other way, and it is essential that you assimilate this fact if your route to success is to be well constructed.

You must understand that it is not a lie to affirm something a certain way which is not as yet physically visible. The mental universe is a senior universe to this physical one which most of us relate to. The mental world is a paragon for this physical world. Spoof Spruce exists etherically in a mental world every bit as physical as the one we build our houses in ... just a little less dense.

This is magic. The Modern Alchemist uses magic to transmute the jigsaw puzzle into the picture which becomes the story. Jigsaw Puzzle Blues only alert a person to the fact that the picture is not taking shape. When human beings are off purpose, *not doing what they want to, not being where they want to be, not working at what they want to be working at, not loving who they want to be loving, not giving what they want to be giving, not taking what they want to be taking* ... the Jigsaw Puzzle Blues appear. There are no words in this song, as they would need to be different for each case. Words to these blues are newly composed by each individual.

If you are not happy, check your story and make the necessary adjustments. Be patient, have faith and determination for all of your wishes to appear ...

An extremely wealthy and successful friend of mine who works in the post production audio business, is sceptical about the power of this mental universe I describe. Yet one day he rushed into a studio in which I was recording, and handed me an envelope from a small pile he was carrying around with him. I opened it and surprise surprise, there was a chain letter, telling me that if I did not send it to another twenty people something dreadful was going to happen to me, as it had to ...

I asked him why he was giving it to me and I could sense the embarrassment. This was an agreement principle with which we were dealing. If enough people believe you to have a million pounds sterling, it is only a matter of time before that happens in the physical world ... that is the law!

Here was somebody hexing my friend, and he was responding ... but ask him to construct his plans deliberately in the mental universe and give them a life usually only thought of as existing in the physical world and he would not ... even though he must be doing exactly that in some way for so many of his plans to achieve fruition.

I binned the letter and broke the chain both mentally and physically, knowing that the mental breaking was the most important aspect for me to accomplish. Ironically enough, and sadly, that friend of mine is now also bankrupt. Chain letters are as powerful as you believe them to be, but let me tell you that anything trading on fear is black magic to say the least, and I advise you to stay clear. It is a more complex subject than at first meets the eye.

By all, means, accumulate agreement on your success, but do not ever use devious tactics. As sure as the tides, what you give you get, and the rebounding onto yourself of previous, less than pleasant outflow, is simple to avoid ...

Outflow goodness ...

AFFIRMATION ... I EMANATE GOODWILL

Thirteen Steps
They're Coming To Take Me Away

Not many people are really able to live exactly as they wish. A series of compromises may be necessary, but one thing you must never compromise with is your own reality ... which is unique to the human being called ... YOU! Realities will change ... adjustments can be made ... improvements should occur ... but compromises shouldn't. They usually result in a half baked attempt at nothing to get nowhere!

This is easy to write about and far harder to execute. You have many forces at work around you. Economics are a tangible issue for most, and possibly a subject which most people can identify with. *Everyone has a price,* states the cliché; how many of us are willing to look beyond short term gain however.

I recently attracted a challenge in the publishing world. I was invited to a meeting at the London offices of a very large multi-national company who had noticed our products, and made their interest in them known to me. This company is big; maybe the biggest in the world for English language material! The first meeting was superficially successful. I was interested in exploring potential interdependence, and they were interested in utilising the same terminology as me to get more sales! I only realised this supposition afterwards.

My concept was that PeRFECT WORDS and MUSIC Limited would remain intact, perhaps under this larger, and I must add quite exciting, umbrella. The potential was vast for both companies, and, as mentioned, the first meeting was promising. The second meeting however, was a sickly affair where eight department chiefs gathered around a table, with me at the head, facing them all. It reminded me of my earlier days playing to club audiences who had not really come to see me in particular; they would fold their arms in a manner which kind of dared me to entertain them, just in case I was good; satisfaction for anyone concerned was rarely accomplished!

So, there I was in front of these employed people who seemed to gain their strength from the company in which they operated. They wanted to know my story. They didn't use those words but it amounts to the same thing. I told them it. They tried to change it as if they knew what was best for us all, which of course they didn't.

The PAC was to become a regular fee paying seminar type activity where books could be almost network marketed. To this proposal I answered in the negative. I proposed that the PAC remain true to its non profit making ideals, but to expand it, along the lines of a discussion group network. This did not smell of profit to the hungry monsters who sat in front of me smelling my every sentence for promotion potential regarding their own stories ... I could sense the atmosphere, which stimulated me to be blatant with my story, rather than the other way round. *Would I run seminars then?* they asked. *No,* I replied, *I am leader of the PAC ... I run the PAC,* I responded. *But there is so much money in seminars and so many books get sold through them.* This rejoicing line was delivered like a coup d'état. They were waiting for me to realise how silly I had been for not understanding this simple tenet of publishing lore.

I was waiting for the end of the meeting. There was still a slight chance of a mutually beneficial future however, until the cards were honestly laid on the table that is ... I told them that I did not believe in seminars anymore. I had surveyed the market place enough to realise that these vastly overpriced ventures made little long term impact on people's lives. They were being used more and more as *the express fix to quick success in sixty seconds by*

awakening the giant wherever he may lurk to realise maximum
achievement of unlimited power by learning seven habits of
principle centred whatsit to do with seeds of greatness before
thinking while you grow rich at everyone else's expense to seeing
it when you believe it thinking what to say when you talk to yourself
after swimming with some sharks!

I didn't say the right things! Oh, I knew what I was doing just as they did. We were not the next episode for each other. They eventually admitted that they really only wanted the first book in my trilogy, *You Can Always Get What You Want* ... it had a proven track record of sales ... it was on more people's wavelength ... it was easy to understand ... it had a catchy title ... IT MADE MONEY!

The fact that it was only the first portion of a three part Body, Mind and Spirit trilogy was irrelevant to them ... they were reluctant to invest in the potential. I told them that I believed ultimately, the title they wanted would sell the least, but the lure of the short term fix was overpowering.

The whole situation reminded me so much of my life in the music business. When I began, record companies invested in the future. The first album from any band or artiste, was merely a taster, the second contained some good songs, the third brought forth one classic and the fourth was full of them. An artist was allowed to breath and develop. This was understood to be a particularly important aspect of real success.

I bet you know who Genesis are!

Did you know their first album called *From Genesis To Revelation* ... the second *Trespass* ... the third *Nursery Crimes* ... the fourth *Foxtrot* ... maybe you remember them.

The point is that it was a long breathing process to get the membership right, the music right, the image right, the everything else right ... then when it seemed to happen Peter Gabriel left!

Now, if it's not *wham bam thank you mam,* someone weird must be at the helm! Singles shoot up the charts, and incidentally rarely make money, performed by artists who frequently end up back at Safeways stacking shelves on the night shift. We are left with an inferior artistic world and nobody really wins. Sure there is an apparency of success, but little signs of a conspiracy. Breathing together means long term gains for all concerned.

Just to finish on the publishing challenge, I was interested to note that the company concerned were also shown on the television programme I mentioned earlier called *Empowerment.* They were taking part in all these childish and wonderful executive games, succeeding on a gruelling physical activity course only to be told with hilarity that they had to start again, and this time complete the same course without shoes. Wild! They talked of the team, but really they feared for there own personal stories. They talked of interdependence but meant control. They flirted with semantics but rarely made the changes brought about through understanding new horizons. This isn't criticism, it is observation. You cannot business develop and expect personal development automatically. Sometimes there is a crossover ... but without regular cognitions about fundamental aspects of this body, mind and spirit world which we inhabit, all these business gurus ever accomplish is a fat personal bank balance while all participants in their programmes become disillusioned before falling back onto old ways and habits. Personal Devastation is what I call it!

I propose that businesses and their gurus should get real about the truth. Stop lying about the authentic reason a business exists ... most usually exist to make money for the owner, and incidentally for the employees to earn an honest living. Exceptions abound ... please do not be offended if you know of one, or if that one is yours. This is a story and can have more impact metaphorically than it does factually ... or vice versa.

My son attends a school which closes the car park entrance as parents arrive in the morning to deliver the pupils. The faculty believe this car park belongs to them. Every day is mayhem, as irritability surfaces whilst mums and dads crawl through the traffic jam trying their best to miss daydreaming pupils who are unaware of all but their passing thoughts. If the entrance was opened, the cars could pass through, drop off the children safely, and leave in an orderly fashion through the exit. Safety in a less than ideal scene! This school must exist solely for the benefit of the teachers ... how annoying it must be to have pupils in their stories at all!

My daughter attends a school which objects to the lunch time assistants being troubled in any way. *Do you know how hard it is to recruit these assistants,* I was told. *What is the purpose of a school and what is your order of importances?* I replied to deaf ears!

That reminds me of the time I became disgusted with the amount of automation which was occurring in the music business for the projection of live performances. Some people, it has to be said, were not even singing live ... they were miming everything! I was using backing tracks and playing live guitar or piano, with a live*ish* vocal performance on top.

I decided I was guilty, and began opening my set of cover material with a piano vocal song. This violated the hit 'em hard with an opening number tenet, and was never particularly successful for me. Rather than returning to the usual blast, to get things going, I decided to strip down my performance even more.

I jettisoned the stage clothes in favour of jeans and a white vest, and axed all backing by beginning with an acappella song. Acappella means singing only! This would win their hearts right from the start, I thought. It is a very difficult way of performing, and I expected lots of respect and admiration from the audience, but it was never forthcoming, mainly because the idea was too far removed from the norm of reverb swamped singing over poorly constructed backing tracks, usually on inferior cassette tape.

Anyway, I felt good about it and an underlying respect crept in over the months during which this attitude was adopted, shattered only when I changed my agent. He rang up one Monday morning, mixing me up with another of his clients, and asked why I was performing songs nobody seemed to know. I corrected him by reviewing a few of my titles for him and he understood that I was not guilty of that particular crime.

Whilst we were talking however, I did mention just how proud I was of the way my opening acappella, then live piano song, was growing in popularity.

Phil, he said, *was that you who was playing at whatsisnames club in Newcastle that Tuesday night about five months ago ... before we took you on?*

Yes! I replied ... recognition from within the business at last, *that was me!*

Drop the acappella at the beginning kidda ... it's crap, he retorted with gusto, *start with something punchy like everyone else!* Gradual Graduation was missing in this little episode from my life!

All around us exist situations that are less than ideal ... muddled stories of interplay between differing realities. Your viewpoint is a living breathing indication of exactly where you are at. It is you ... you are it. The interplay between viewpoints is called life.

Choose good viewpoints like you would pick your clothes. Update them as you would a data base. Share them for the benefit of all, and when your reality comes across a less ethical one ... do not compromise. Evolve!

AFFIRMATION ... I AM COMMITTED TO MY EVOLVING
REALITY

Fourteen Steps
The Supernatural Anaesthetist

Few things can be more debilitating than the natural cycle of
Inspire, Perform and Receive, being curtailed, suppressed or
interrupted in some aberrant way. You get the idea, which is *the
inspiration,* you act on it, this is *the performance,* and then you
accept the inevitable inflow which is *the receiving.* If this is
interrupted, the consequences can be dire; bodily, mentally and
spiritually. We could also say *Inspire, Perspire until you Conspire,
then open your arms for the forthcoming result.* Do you agree?
The 1+1=3 theory tells us that sharing makes humans more
powerful.

1+1 can sometimes equal 0 also; it depends who the 1 is that
you are sharing with. You can be stopped bodily by a burly human
who is being his chest. You can be stopped mentally, by a human
so filled with knowledge that his *tao,* or *way,* cannot be seen for
data litter. There is also The Supernatural Anaesthetist, who
occasionally appears to dampen your most enlightened aspirations
with a quick injection of cosmic chloroform.

What can I say to help with such opportunities?

Tao Te Ching, which in English means *The Book of the Way,*
was composed by the Chinese mystic and sage *Lao Tzu.* I recently
and fortuitously ran into the following set of words thanks to a
Buddhist friend of mine called Glo. They fit in with my own TTM
philosophy, and frequently can be helpful to those of us who
inevitably get caught up in the seriousness of this living game of
which we are all partaking.
Taoist Reflection

Close your eyes and you will see clearly
Cease to listen and you will hear truth
Be silent and your heart will sing
Seek no contacts and you will find union
Be still and you will move forward on the tide of spirit
Be gentle and you will need no strength
Be patient and you will achieve all things
Be humble and you will remain entire

Wise words require little explanation and much contemplation. The Supernatural Anaesthetist cannot interfere with realistic aspirations emanating from a clean being. A frequent story is told of why Christ had only one set of clothes; it was because dirt cannot stick to such purity. I believe in paragons and the quality reported to have been brought forth by The Christ is certainly something to aim for; yet in the same breath, I must add that it would be unrealistic to expect immediate elevation in all that you do and say, up to the standards exhibited by this remarkable being around two thousand years ago.

If you begin to expect too much, The Supernatural Anaesthetist may appear to settle you into a perhaps superficially undesirable sleep ... much as an alcoholic sleeps off the beer, you may awake to a more realistic aim!

It is not in my nature to evaluate what goes on in another's universe. In fact I consider evaluation by others to be the single most antagonistic opponent to true cognition and self realisation. Yet, evaluation is rife. Psychiatrists are perhaps the worst offenders; they should be forgiven however, for they work with a science so incomplete and splattered with inconsistencies, I am surprised anyone uses them; but use them they do do do!

I am more interested in everyday life. Habits can be changed more quickly in regular situations ... if I start criticising the psychiatric profession it could be dangerous. Vested interests have peculiar habits related to getting their own way through influence.

What is evaluation?

I use it to mean *determining someone else's situation through your own eyes; value judgements; appraising a situation of which you can understand nothing objectively, for someone else who can comprehend totally if encouraged and given the chance!*

Most magazine type television programmes have a resident agony aunt, understanding uncle, psychiatrist, psychologist, sociologist or presenter, and they all seem eager when it comes to offering advice. My advice is for them to stop it! It is a very dangerous practice and the patient frequently *becomes* the advice. In plainer words, when you advise someone, they sometimes hold onto that advice as an excuse ... tell someone they are stressed and they may become stressed ... suggest that they should cut down on alcohol and they could become alcoholic ... tell them to *snap out of it* and they may just snap into it, not having realised the possibility existed that they were *in it* in the first place.

This is a superficial treatment of what is possibly one the most significant salient points of these 49 steps. By all means utilise others for stimulation, but always hold your own council. No other person knows better than you about you.

I really like him ... do you think I'm stupid? I always worry about everything ... do you think I'm crazy? I'm easily swayed ... do you think I'm normal? I don't bear grudges ... do you think I should? The list could continue for many more pages as you can well imagine.

All of these questions are so subjective. Does it matter what another thinks of your operating mechanisms? No, it doesn't! Don't confuse this advice with the seeking of factual information on house buying, finance, building and other everyday issues. Or for that matter, proven factual information to do with how the mind works, or the spirit or the body. That is different. Make the distinction and stop asking others what they would do if they were in your situation ... they just do not know because they are not in it.

All this has little to connect it with The Supernatural Anaesthetist however, except perhaps a notion that it is better to be calmed by this cosmic figure because of your unrealistically high aspirations, than it is to spend your life running around asking others to evaluate your life for you.

The new age is as guilty as the old age of this crime ... perhaps more so. With a little help from The Supernatural Anaesthetist's colleague, who calls herself The Universal Knower, we too can become omniscient, and then get on with the far more important task of seeking wisdom within ... a task which has little relating it to knowledge.

AFFIRMATION ... I HOLD MY OWN COUNCIL

Reflection ...

New ways are not necessarily easy to assimilate into an otherwise orderly life. The 49 steps is not a course with a beginning, a middle and a diploma at the end. This is a book which you will need to live with, explore alongside, discard if need be, exalt if it grabs you that way; but whatever you do, please do not allow this opportunity to pass by like the reading of an entertaining novel. I will have wasted your time and mine; most importantly you will have wasted your own time and mine.

Continuing with the theme of esoteric correspondence between the seven levels in this book, and years in a person's life; between the age of eight and fourteen a human being would be occupied, albeit subconsciously for the most part, with the building of its Desire Body. This body is frequently referred to as the Astral Body, with which a person works to get what they want. This Astral Body however, frequents the mentioned world of desire, along with the astral representations of the majority of humanity. It is an uncontrolled world of grab and run, take and take, duplicity, hidden agendas and personalities snatching the glamour, as opposed to characters living their stories.

Sadly, many people do not aspire beyond this world, and therein lies the problem in many a dispute between brothers and sisters of this universe. Do not get trapped! Remember that this stage corresponds with puberty and adolescence; a stage to be enjoyed and transcended.

Explore the story, give it a twist, make it magnetic, charge it with purpose, line it with silk, inject it with truth, and above all ... begin to live it! Another story you may wish to survey, is an excellent book called The Tao of Pooh, by Benjamin Hoff ... in which The Way is revealed by the Bear of Little Brain!

AFFIRMATIONS

WHATEVER I THINK I AM, I AM ... I CAN CHANGE MY CIRCUMSTANCES ... I SEE ALL AS OPPORTUNITY ... I HAVE A HEALTHY BODY ... I EMANATE GOODWILL ... I AM COMMITTED TO MY EVOLVING REALITY ... I HOLD MY OWN COUNCIL

Get the picture of your goal just how you want it, and hold that idea in your mind until it becomes a physical reality. Mix emotion with desire, formulate a plan, mix the ingredients together, then go and make it happen ...

Phil Murray; *You Can Always Get What You Want*

The Advanced PAC Practitioner

Abou Ben Adhem

Abou Ben Adhem (may his tribe increase!)
Awoke one night from a deep dream of peace,
And saw, within the moonlight in his room,
Making it rich, like a lily in bloom,
An angel writing in a book of gold:
Exceeding peace had made Ben Adhem bold,
And to the presence in the room he said,
"What writest thou?" - The vision raised its head,
And, with a look made of all sweet accord,
Answered, "The names of those who love the Lord."
"And is mine one?" said Abou. "Nay, not so,"
Replied the angel. Abou spoke more low,
But cheerily still; and said, "I pray thee, then,
Write me as one that loves his fellowmen."
The angel wrote, and vanished. The next night
It came again, with a great wakening light,
And showed the names whom love of god had blessed, -
And lo! Ben Adhem's name led all the rest.

James Leigh Hunt

Fifteen Steps

Kahu The Kahuna

Harry Smith had dreamt of Hawaii.

Now that he had reached the peak of his power in the world of business, he was able to live wherever he wanted, and he wanted Hawaii. Unfortunately, the authorities would not grant Harry a long stay visa. He had the necessary funds and credentials; but he also had a conviction for smoking marijuana in public during a nineteen sixties Notting Hill Carnival. He was a teenager at the time and didn't give a fig for the future, and now that future was here.

Why was I so stupid, he repeated to himself time and time again like a backward, negative affirmation, *why was I so stupid?*

Harry was used to getting his own way and no short sighted bureaucracy would stop him; not now; not ever. He entered Hawaii with a visitors visa on a stop over to Sydney, Australia. The thing is he didn't leave again and that was three years ago. Excusing the odd hiccup and near collision with authority, they had been the best three years of his eventful life.

Never married, no children and now no family whatsoever to speak of, Harry felt himself to be master of his own destiny. There were a few odd second cousins, coincidentally living in Australia for where he had purchased that air ticket which allowed him to slip through the USA immigration net in Hawaii, but they didn't count. He was scared to contact them in case they smelled his money, and plenty of that particular form of energy he certainly had.

Harry had decided to go it alone. Money helped him with that choice and he was a firm believer in buying the future. He was well read, university educated, self motivated, a keen golfer, knew everything there was to know about the Futures Market of The London Stock Exchange, but by no stretch of a creative imagination could anyone describe him as well liked. Not even liked for that matter.

He was in fact a small bodied selfish man, dedicated to himself and all that self gratification had to offer. He would have married himself and had himself as his child if that was the way; it wasn't so he made do with but one of this fabulous creation called Harry Smith. He couldn't get enough of Harry; he drank alone, swam alone, thought alone, invested alone, had sex alone and talked to himself.

There he was at the turn of the millennium, out in the wilds of Hawaii, just as he had dreamed all those years before ... *why was I so stupid,* he repeated to himself time and time again as a continuing negative affirmation, *why was I so stupid ...* the thought of himself smoking pot all those years ago in swinging London certainly had left an indelible imprint on his psyche. Others recalled the synthetic awakening of new horizons rarely to be sensed again without the drug stimulus; Harry recalled the stupidity. That was Harry ... no profit no point.

The raging fashion had been to find the weirdest way of seeing in the twenty first century and Harry had chosen a party by a volcano, miles from Honolulu, which peaked at midnight as everyone walked over the red hot coals. It was midnight plus and the party was over; it was over for Harry anyway. He refused to walk the coals and cursed the organiser, who looked like he was a native Polynesian Hawaiian. The offence was noted by everyone, the party soured and his money pouch mysteriously disappeared, along with the transport which was to have returned him to civilisation in Honolulu.

Why was I so stupid? Talk about superstitious, he said out aloud to himself, *those damned natives always take everything so seriously!*

How do you know, came the reply from behind, *are you such an expert on us natives?* As the voice spoke, its body pushed Harry's to the ground and began kicking it. Harry screamed out but no one heard. The party was over. *What do you want?* he demanded. *All you have,* came the reply as his wallet was stolen and he was stripped naked.

He could not see who to blame for his predicament. The light was poor and transient, as cloud suppressed any power the moonbeams had. *You think we are superstitious,* said his assailant, *here take this photograph, you should recognise that it is taken from a painting of someone you will recognise, as the clouds clear and light is available; the only way you will get down this mountain alive is by praying to the photograph. I know who you are Harry Smith; you are an illegal alien who thinks of us as those damned natives. If you contact the Police I guarantee you will be deported. I further suggest the possibility that your assets in Hawaii will be frozen when the authorities here are tipped off that you have been working and not paying taxes ... even though you haven't!*

Why are you doing this to me? asked Harry meekly.

For three reasons Harry, replied the voice, *firstly you cursed the Kahuna who was there to help you conquer the heat from the coals, secondly I don't like you, and thirdly I wish to teach you a lesson. I suggest that you start praying as you walk ... that a way.*

The thief pointed in a general direction then disappeared, and Harry began walking. His groin ached from a well aimed kick, and after three hours of walking, hobbling, stream crossing and cursing his predicament, the cloud cleared and he viewed the photograph which mysteriously for Harry, he had not thrown away with a curse; rather he had clutched at it all the way down the mountain. It was torn and folded. Harry cried for the first time in his adult life. His body could take no more. Still naked, he was cold from both shock and temperature, hungover from the alcohol, and for the first time since being mugged, he was frightened of what could happen to him as he continued down the mountain. Horror stories crossed his mind and he began to consider the options.

Here take this photograph, you will see that it is taken from a painting of someone you will recognise ... the words haunted him ... he could walk no further and thought he heard footsteps in the distance ... *the only way you will get down this mountain alive is by praying to the photograph.*

Harry believed in himself; he recognised Jesus on the photograph in classic pose, walking amongst the people. Under normal circumstances he would have laughed at the notion of praying to this idea of Jesus, but he could now see a figure walking towards him. Clouds once again suppressed the light as he got down on his knees. He placed the photograph as close to his eyes as eyelashes would permit, and said quietly ... *oh Lord, you probably do not know me as I have always been a non believer ... not any more ... please help me ... someone is walking towards me, I fear for my life ... please let this person be friendly ... please have whoever it is help me.*

He hid the photograph from view by once again clutching it in his hand, and rose from his knees. The person who had made the sound of footsteps earlier drew alongside in silence. Harry didn't know what to say and the stranger didn't need to say anything, so he once again began to walk, leaving Harry looking on in wonder. Harry shouted after him ... help me please! The stranger returned and gave Harry his jacket and hat. *Happy New Year my friend ... although it does not look like it has been so far for you. What happened to you?*

Harry related the story of his mugging, and even confessed his prayer to the photograph. The stranger understood and sympathised while guiding Harry to a car which was parked not 100 metres from where they had met. It seems Harry had been descending the volcano on a rough path which had probably run parallel to the highway for the previous two hours of his stamina trial. Harry cursed to himself and the stranger kindly drove him home to his Honolulu mansion.

Aren't you curious as to why this all happened to you? asked the stranger who called himself Kahu. Harry now guessed him to be of Arab descent.

Why can you tell me? Harry replied cynically, now that he was back in the safety of his own home.

I am from the Atlas mountains in Africa, began the stranger, *many moons ago, and long before your Jesus Christ who you say is on this photograph, my people felt that it was time to travel and spread their word to farther corners of our earth.*

Harry was visibly impatient but answered negatively when his rescuer asked if he'd had enough.

Well, he continued, *it was the Huna which they feared for. The Huna is the Secret; it is the meaning of life ... and the Huna was guarded and kept alive by the Kahuna. Verbally passed from Kahuna to trainee Kahuna over many thousands of years, the Huna was a method by which one was able to contact the higher self, which only becomes active when commanded. This was the secret of healing, miracles, weather control and success; but also of death, destruction, failure and many more negative phenomena. The Kahuna had few scruples however, and the ethical codes were strictly connected to survival ... they certainly would not be tolerated in this new twenty first century, or by modern, western civilisation. Anyway, the Kahuna guided large numbers of Atlas Mountain dwellers in open boats, thousand of miles in what seemed like as many months, and settled in this South Pacific triangle known as Polynesia ... from here in Hawaii all the way down to New Zealand and across to Tahiti, the immigrants settled and the Kahunas ensured the survival of the Huna. All food was provided by the Kahuna connection to their higher selves and the weather spirits were asked to be kind, as was the great spirit of the sea. The sun looked after them and limited its solar power lest it injure any one of them. It was indeed a miracle.*

Where do you fit in? Harry asked with a snigger.

The last Hawaiian Kahuna departed this mortal coil in the year 1900, and Polynesia has been without for one hundred years. It was the law that should this ever happen, another Kahuna would be dispatched from the Atlas Mountains to reinstate this essential continuance of Huna Power.

Harry was tired and grew rude and irritable ... *that's why you're here, you are just about to tell me?*

That is correct, the stranger replied without rising to Harry's cynicism, *I have come to help!*

Listen Ka Ka or whatever your name is, thanks for the lift. Here's twenty dollars that should see you alright, Harry pushed a note roughly into Kahu's hand, *I've never been a one for those far fetched superstitious stories but thanks anyway.* Harry opened the door, but Kahu was offended.

Don't you recognise me? asked Kahu, *I was the one you cursed when you did not have the courage to walk the coals, even though that was a commitment made by all who attended the party. Your perception of reality is so weak you do not even recognise me as the one who attacked you and robbed you of this wallet.*

Kahu threw the wallet onto the table in mild anger, but continued.

I said we knew the Secret; I did not say that we were passive peace lovers. The contrary is frequently the case. We live in a violent world. You only recognised me as your rescuer and even now you are irritable and trying to rid yourself of my presence. You call me superstitious my friend, but let me ask you to do one thing before I leave ... where is that photograph I gave you after I kicked your groin?

Harry picked up the photograph from the floor and looked

again. His face changed expression from cynical irritation into a contorted scowl.

That is right my friend, your eyes do not deceive you this time. You prayed to a photograph of me. In one night, you cursed me, were attacked by me, rescued by me, and you even prayed to me.

I, Kahu The Kahuna, ask you my friend, who do you now think is the superstitious one?

AFFIRMATION...I AM TOLERANT OF OTHER VIEWPOINTS

Sixteen Steps
> Twenty First Century Schizoid Man

We are all a bit schizophrenic; we hallucinate and suffer from frequent delusions of one kind or another. We have varying periods of lost contact with reality and occasionally we think that we are somebody else. Some just hope they will become someone else.

Where will this world take us? The above description sounds like it is time to batten down the hatches and wait for calmer weather. Not so however! Twenty First Century Schizoid Man has an opportunity that no previous wave of evolution's humanity has had. We have the chance to adopt new principles which up until now would have appeared weak and flimsy. Many philosophies connect humanity too closely with that of the animal world. Hence the theory that man's purpose is to survive, which is rubbish.

Man *can* survive, and if that was the purpose for living we would now all be dead from terminal boredom. The purpose of humanity is to evolve, and the very definition of that word means change. Twenty First Century Schizoid Man has the opportunity to make a giant leap ahead by agreeing to leave behind all those unworkable and old fashioned Piscean ways, in favour of the new Aquarian potential. We then become Twenty First Century

Humanity, a caring society of Advanced PAC Practitioners.

This does not mean that we leave ambition behind ... without that we would be dead also. It does mean that we stop paying lip service to groovy philosophies and begin to live them if they are of any use. If you would like some concrete descriptions of what the future may have in store for us, then Alvin Toffler seems to have a finger on that type of prediction. This will appeal to the sociologists and organisers in our midst, and is essential for societal forward planning.

I deal with individual forward planning, present time living and only occasional past time handlings. With now and the future in mind, I offer you a formula. I concocted this recipe from my own story, and mixed it together with much research that I have undertaken of nineteenth and twentieth century success literature. It makes good reading and I guarantee its practicability. I believe in a pragmatic approach to most of what we contact during the living of our wonderfully varied stories.

An Advanced PAC Practitioner, is a person with a vision. PAC is an acronym for Positive Attitude Club, which is a non profit making organisation dedicated to peaceful interdependence, creative discussion and forward thinking for the World. The PAC Philosophy states simply that improvement of personal life through positive attitudes, benefits Humanity as a Whole. Yet again we are dealing with an evolving principle. It is for this reason that we are less attractive to those amongst us who like regimentation and a well defined world. The PAC is both a concept we can carry with us wherever our stories take us, and a physical organisation of people who are joined by a regular newsletter, some of whom attend the actual meetings.

There are few rules, but we do stress the creative discussion aspect of our purpose when we meet. We are not a therapy group and do not handle individual problems. They are for the individual to handle, who, having handled them, may wish to join in with the creative discussion which is available *because* we don't get involved with personal problems, challenges or opportunities.

This is the formula that takes the Schizoid out of Twenty First Century Man.

Good luck, and may you never be the same again!

THE 21st CENTURY SUCCESS FORMULA

1 Know your story and conceive a long term plan for it
2 Formulate a method for the accomplishment of that plan
3 Check your intentions for integrity and make any necessary adjustments
4 Reformulate your plan with a sound budget and realistic short term targets
5 Become sensitive to interdependence possibilities
6 Dedicate your outlook to positive attitudes
7 Encapsulate your complete visualisation into a succinct sentence which can be called your Mission Statement
8 Be definite about everything that you do in connection with your mission
9 Learn from your mistakes
10 Maintain a relevant level of physical fitness
11 Encourage inner enthusiasm
12 Have faith in your future
13 Insist on self discipline and intuitive ethics
14 Always give over and above what is expected of you
15 Acknowledge your connection to the universe and begin a trusting relationship with it
16 Use TTM, an acronym for time to myself, as an essential part of your process
17 Practice mastery over your own mind and thought patterns
18 Reformulate your plan
19 Surround yourself with a supergroup of like minded people
20 Live life with an outgoing smile and an inner knowingness

AFFIRMATION ... I PLEDGE MYSELF TO MY SUCCESS

Seventeen Steps
                    Across The Universe

The Aquarian Conspiracy is a book written by Marilyn Ferguson, describing the emergence of an apparently unco-ordinated number of interactive and interdependent individuals, forming a network powerful enough to instigate radical, new and more relevant operating procedures through the creation of a different type of society than that of which we are presently cognisant. It is leaderless, and is based on a wider vision of human potential. It is worth reading and quite naturally I recommend it as another step towards *Pan Awareness.*

I was mostly unaware of this rise in public opinion at grass roots level, when I wrote *You Can Always Get What You Want,* and offered ... *an open invitation to join the PAC; a brand new concept for connecting the Force of POSITIVE THINKERS throughout the World.* The PAC however, put me in touch with this feeling which is bubbling under much of society, and placed me directly in contact with many other people who are forming themselves into groups for the purpose of furthering the cause of Human Potential. This movement, I must point out has been gathering momentum since before I was born.

I always think of it as beginning around 1875 with the emergence of Madame Blavatsky, but I feel that it caught mass awareness in the 1930's with the emergence of the Human Potential Movement, which is still with us, and will probably shoulder much responsibility for the easing of the Aquarian Age mores into society. Now, what I further discovered, and this is important, was that many if not most of the people connected to research, living, or, flirting with human potential, did not necessarily have positive attitudes about what they were doing.

Just like the rest of society, the new age comprised of just as wide a spectrum of human viewpoint as the old age had. Also, the PAC did not necessarily attract positive minded people. We soon discovered, at the first meeting in fact, when a member spoke of himself as being the most negative minded person he knew, that we needed the negative to stimulate the positive. That great law of correspondence would not spare us, and we now understand that the PAC is a growth group of a wide variety of people attracted to it for as wide a spectrum of reasons.

So, we are not a group of smiley, mouth open, half witted failures who bleat on about the wonderful world of PAC; we are only what we are at a given time. The PAC is different at each meeting, and quite naturally I encourage the formation of as many local PACs as possible. The PAC is a non profit making organisation. Maintaining the sixth sense of humour firmly to the forefront of our thinking, we pronounce it PACK, and in keeping with the founder's entertainment background, Phil Murray is *Leader of the PAC*.

We meet regularly at our base in the South East of England, and less frequently elsewhere. The PAC is therefore, a physical actuality, but more importantly, it is a concept which can be carried with you, whatever your circumstances and wherever you may be. The philosophy states simply that *improvement of personal life through positive attitudes, benefits humanity as a whole*. We believe that forward thinking through creative discussion for the World and immediate surroundings alike, is a service. This does not amount to a glib interpretation of positivity being permanent smiles, and replying affirmatively to every question asked. The philosophy is not about the blind rendition of irritating platitudes like *think positively* and *keep smiling,* at inopportune times. It is about finding the *win for all ingredient* when dealing with others.

It is about living the talk of your beliefs, and demonstrating an understanding that before any beginning is a thought!

People matter most!

Anyone who feels that we fulfil a role relevant to the particular process which they are currently undergoing as a human being seems to be attracted, and some join. In practical terms, this means that we have a membership of people from all walks of life. There is no hierarchy, condescending attitude or patronisation of *less advanced* viewpoints. There is a tolerance of all, and an understanding that the quickest way to learn is by teaching what you know.

Many people have tired of old ways which may include the regimentation and categorising of anything that moves. Some people embrace the philosophy but do not join up; this is entirely in keeping with our purpose. Others do not join because they consider our one enrollment condition, which asks that you believe *positive attitudes to be helpful,* is not so. We do not refuse anyone initially, and certainly don't push our views antagonistically onto people in an effort to make them join. The PAC is a service and not a hindrance. It will exist for two hundred years, during which time many will come and go ... the service however, will evolve! Joining the PAC does not give you a positive attitude; only you can grant this state of mind personally! If you decide to bestow this quality onto yourself, we believe that this is beneficial to others also.

Many acts of service are invisible; it is for individuals to decide how best to serve themselves and humanity alike. This assumes that you have cognited on the teaching of ageless wisdom which states that *it is impossible to be a great giver and also unsuccessful.* Some PAC People engage in acts of charity, others give mentally, and a number combine both exoteric and esoteric varieties of service. The occasional person joins before realising that it is not a *grab everything you can* club full of *personalities;* they soon loose interest, but at times return when the PAC fulfills a newly awakened role within their lives.

We wrote letters to encourage the cessation of hostilities in Northern Ireland and letters to discourage the French Nuclear tests of 1995, just as some of us meditate encouraging the manifestation of *light, love and power* on the planet. The PAC also believes in happiness, enjoyment, financial success and material wealth, during the accomplishment of an individual's spiritual aims and aspirations. We believe in goals, and encourage knowledge of the relevant tools which will ensure an enjoyable execution of the intent. The PAC is a concept which can form the foundation for many varying themes; there are no religious barriers, and a fundamental theosophical axiom at the base of our modus operandi states that *there is no religion higher than truth!* The PAC always seeks practical applications inherent in every theory!

Words flow easily and are doing so across the universe. There are groups all over the world getting together for a variety of purposes. There seems to be an underlying sentiment with most of them however; it is that human potential grows in ratio to the amount of attention that is placed on it.

This is precisely what the PAC accomplishes.

It stimulates PAC Peoples' attention onto potential.

AFFIRMATION ... I EXPLORE MY POTENTIAL

Eighteen Steps
                    You Only Live Twice

In any one lifetime you can be conscious of what is and what could be. An Advanced PAC Practitioner is aware of this and understands there is one life for now and one for dreams. You only

82

live twice and I suggest to you that it is time to begin *documenting* a route to success. Remember that all success is a conspiracy of one kind or another ... who are you going to breathe with?

Compose your Ten Commitments for a bright life. I offer a sample ...

The Ten Commitments

1 I devote one hour per week to *the plan* for my success.
2 I help myself and others through being affluent
3 I conspire with my colleagues for our mutual success
4 I investigate new areas of activity
5 I relax
6 I encourage my colleagues
7 I only undertake ethical ventures
8 I use TTM
9 I commit to be fit
10 I endeavour to be happy

You may feel that the above sentiments are a little lightweight. You must compose your own, which inevitably will fit into your reality level. As we have now reached a stage of documentation, it is also time to consider recording exactly what your story is. In my earlier work I called this composing a Mission Statement, and followed it with a Visualisation Statement.

In The 49 Steps it is writing a synopsis of your story, and embodying in one succinct sentence, exactly what your story is about. As all stories are living and breathing entities with lives of their own, so your sentence embodiment will have to change and evolve with circumstances and physical universe life. There is no such thing as a completed story that I am aware of ... episodes come and go ... chapters close and others open ... characters do well while their colleagues suffer ... plots can mislead ... and what about the twist?

The story needs regular attention and the plan which supports it is right at the very beginning of the Ten Commitments ... *I devote one hour per week to the plan for my success.* We must separate the plan from the story however, as the story is forever; the plan is but an episode.

I will now share with you my story ...

Using the medium of entertainment, I am dedicated to the act of providing enjoyment, increasing awareness, and learning to appreciate the natural talent that lies within both myself and others.

It is quite a few years since this story has changed. You may notice that it mentions nothing about writing personal development books or recording successful audio cassette tape programmes. This information is too specific for the story encapsulated into one succinct sentence. It comes later in the plan. Wouldn't it be convenient if we were able to have our stories written onto our calling cards ... *have gun will travel ... licensed to kill.*

Potential colleagues would be able to inspect your card to interpret your story and see if it connects up with theirs. Trust would play a great part in this ... many people would not wish to record their story in case it stopped them getting on. Of course ultimately it would only stop you from engaging yourself in an activity incompatible with your story.

That reminds me of my acting days where it was thought morally acceptable to tell all sorts of lies in order to land the part. We frequently had to record our special skills onto application forms, and there was not an actor I knew who could not scuba dive, parachute, fly jet aircraft, do moon landings and horseride. This last skill, or lack of it, once caught up with me when I was chosen for a part in a BBC series because of this ability, which I said I had but didn't.

I got the part and hastily booked a lesson at a stable on the

Ashdown Forest in East Sussex. The teacher was disgusted because I arrived in tight jeans and cowboy boots ... *my interpretation of the right image,* which was completely wrong. I could not mount the horse let alone ride it. Anyway, the following day we were shooting down at Bodium Castle, a stunning location ideal for the medieval scene in which I played a Squire.

My horse was a trained mare who knew that she had to rear onto her hind legs when commanded to do so. The first scene involved her trainer shouting this order from the bushes. She reared, I almost fell off, and the trainer took me to one side ... *you can't ride can you,* he stated knowingly ... *no, I confessed, please look after me ... it's best that the director doesn't know!*

Thank goodness he wasn't a *jobsworth.* He looked after me and I learned some basics about horse riding, whilst exhibiting the advanced skills of a stuntman! Worse came later when I had to draw my sword as I was attacked. The worry was always that if I was thrown, my feet, which were swathed in medieval rags to keep them warm, would jam in the stirrups and I would end up being dragged from the set like a scene from a western. The final hour of that day was spent trotting down a tarmac lane, the tarmac not in shot, accompanying *My Lord.* It had been raining and the horse slipped all over the place. What seemed like an easy conclusion to this lie ended by being the hardest to accomplish. Every time the horse slipped I felt like I was falling off. With each slip by the horse, I would instinctively grab the horses neck and the director would shout cut. I eventually ran out of excuses as the light was fading, and we managed to get the shot finished only because I utilised willpower to refrain from automatic response.

Commercials are a lucrative option for actors, and more lies are told in an effort to land them, than anything else I know. The most blatant lie I ever told was during an audition, following an invitation to act in a follow up commercial to the original ... *which I had been in.* The production company was the same for both commercials, but I did not recognise any of the personnel, and I had been given the audition through a different agent to the previous time.

The word went round the waiting room that they would use no actor who had advertised anything in the previous three years. I was on camera, the audition was smooth and I felt right for the part ... *didn't we all* ... then the ten thousand pound question was asked ... *Phil, answer to camera please, have you advertised any other product over the last three years?*

Nothing, I replied convincingly.

Rubbish, came a response from behind a glare of the lights, *you were in the last one we did for this product.*

Ah, I thought you meant apart from that, I lied ...

I've seen you in others too ...

I was waiting for the cliché *don't call us, we'll call you,* which I think in my case would have been, *don't call us and we'll not call you!*

They understood the situation, but all of these lies flying about did make an unhealthy situation of the casting process. I ceased telling these so called professional lies after that embarrassing experience. I remembered the feeling of being caught out and had no wish to repeat it thank you!

Can entertain ... will travel.

I don't think the climate is always healthy enough to include your story on a calling card, but if it is in your story, do it!

The plan which follows the story is a different beingness and we must therefore treat it accordingly. I share with you my plan which has changed greatly over the years ...

The Plan

I write quality songs, plays, novels, articles, success literature and inspirational material.

I record quality songs, music and inspirational material.

I research and write success formulae and goal techniques.

I am a successful focaliser

I have an expanding readership and listenership

I interdepend with Perfect Words and Music Limited, as a vehicle for myself and others.

I have recognition within the entertainment and publishing industries.

I am a best selling writer.

I am known as an artist of quality and integrity.

I write stories that people enjoy.

I am a successful person.

I am a strong family oriented person.

I am a good husband and father.

I enjoy life to the full.

Notice the continuous utilisation of the present tense for reason already mentioned and once again affirmed here by repetition. You must state that your life is already the way you wish it to be. Doing this harnesses the power of the sub conscious mind to ensure that things are exactly the way you have described them. If you say circumstances will eventually be a particular way then that is what will be acknowledged by your sub conscious ... and things will always be in the future, never manifesting in the now!

Spend some time right now, affirming your current success ... *I am wealthy ... I am successful ... I earn in excess of 100,000 per year ... I earn this money from many enjoyable sources ... people like my work ... I am popular ... I am good at my job ... I am a good father ... I am a good husband ... I always have time for my Family ... I always have time for my friends ... I have a second home in Florida ... I own two new cars ... my wife does not need to work ... I give a lot to charity ... I always keep 10% of my income ... my income is always increasing ... I enjoy being rich ... being rich allows me to be more spiritual ... I am constantly improving myself spiritually ... I like myself ... I like myself ... I like myself!*

AFFIRMATION ... MY AFFIRMATIONS WORK WELL FOR ME

Nineteen Steps

Rubber Ball

In business, every Advanced PAC Practitioner knows that outflow equals inflow. That inflow is not necessarily directly related to the outflow, except that it is following the law which states that energy expended will always equal energy accumulated ... *eventually!* Now anyone engaged in even basic business will know simple statistics like ... *only ever expect a less than 5% response to a mail shot, and that's if you're lucky!*

How does outflow equal inflow here. It doesn't on the face of it, but we are not looking at life superficially. Just like the rubber ball that always bounces back to you, business relies on an amount of initial force for propulsion. The ball will only return to you if aimed accurately wherever you bounce it, and in a direct line on which you desire it to return. Now you can place the same force into the bounce of that ball as you did on the previous occasion, only this time angle it, and watch it smash the green house glass. If that glass belongs to next door then you will have to be satisfied with the inflow being anger from your neighbour.

So, outflow does equal inflow, but this equation is so simple that we must embroider it. Quality of outflow equals quality of inflow. Aimless outflow equals random inflow. Outflow your rubbish and inflow someone else's rubbish.

Well, kind of ... it seems that this simple equation is bound up in so many other computations that we can only really utilise it as a rule of thumb, or as a generality. It is fair to say that if you keep on putting good flows outward, you will attract flows of a similar quality back to you. People frequently quote stories of model citizens who are stabbed to death outside the hospice they are just about to donate their life savings to, and ask if this is fair. Fair or not it is irrelevant. We cannot tell what goes on life in life out across someone else's universe. We do not know what karmic muddle our good neighbour is in, or indeed and more relevantly, we do not usually know the ins and outs of our own karmic situation.

I always use the outflow equals inflow equation in connection with my energy output and inflow. I have noted that an imbalance either way can cause gross physiological reactions in a human being. You cannot keep putting out without contravening a universal law ... unless you balance the scales yourself, your inflow could amount to sickness. Balance is the order of this Age in which we live ... not too much of anything at any time. If your outs and ins are balanced, then so should be your physical health, and the well being of your business, whatever that may be.

Your business has a story, as has every little thing in the cosmos. You do not have to be self employed for qualification to inflow this information. It does not matter who your business belongs to ... you are part of its story and it is part of yours. I have a limited company called Perfect Words and Music. We have a digital studio and publish a variety of material. We often get propositioned in various ways, and we are able to stay on track by referring to our story. I know that it is fashionable to invite everyone's participation in the formulation of such stories, but I believe that the initial vision must be conceived by usually one and occasionally two people.

The story can change with the personnel, but it is my

experience that most people are uncommitted to other owned businesses and are apt to throw them off course with casual suggestion and ill informed guidance. With no vision of any personal vested interest, an individual is not likely to tune into the first draft of your businesses story by offering an even more suitable second draft. I suggest care, and each time you find yourself excluding other people's ideas, reaffirm your commitment to both those people, and externally generated good ideas for your business.

The story for my business is this ...

Through publishing, recording and live performance, we are dedicated to the service of quality works and artistes, with the aim of enjoyment and enhancement for the world as a whole, whilst improving the fortune, and excellence of life, for everyone concerned with PeRFECT WORDS and MUSIC Limited

The plan currently is that ...

We honestly and successfully market quality works and artistes, worldwide.
We provide a secure and enjoyable working environment for all employees.
We always see our business as being long term.
We never ever take short cuts to the detriment of a product.
We are seen as an honest and successful company in the entertainment industry.
We are involved in many aspects of the entertainment and personal development industries.
We are innovative.
We are helpful to others within the business world.
We are wealthy market leaders.
We maintain dignity at all times.

AFFIRMATION ... I KNOW MY STORY
Twenty Steps

Leader Of The PAC

That's me!

It isn't everyone who notices the humour in this title. Of course it is taken from the pop song and I hope you can see that it is also tongue in cheek. I am not a *self styled guru,* as one newspaper described me, and I have no interest whatsoever in forming any mysterious group based around nonsense ritual and superstition. We do have this type of preconceived idea to deal with however.

Some people need to reassure themselves that we are not some loony fringe group who exist only to recruit members for a larger parent organisation through brainwashing. Coincidentally, I happen to live in an extremely active geographical area from a spiritual perspective, and this makes the PAC all the more open to misunderstanding.

Let me be quite unambiguous about the fact that the Positive Attitude Club is a totally independent group who seek interdependence with suitable groups. This interdependence is currently quite hard to come by, but I remain convinced that it is a way of the future available in the now. Trust and trustworthiness are the main ingredients needed for such coexistence to become agreeable for more and more people, and they are available in increasing quantities; as people place attention on these possibilities, so do they come into physical manifestation. Just as war comes about through an amount of attention being given over to it ... so does peace. John Lennon knew that and devoted considerable amounts of his time to the simple cause of ending all wars and starting all peace. Declare peace and stop war!

Remember that whatever you have your attention on, is a direct reflection of where you are at as a human being. You are your viewpoint and it is easy to assess a person's evolutionary state by the stories that are told by that individual ... *we are the stories we tell!*

I am currently telling the PAC story and *it* is in its infancy. We are evolving ... discovering ways to become more useful.

Exploring potential that exists all around us. Inspiring and motivating all that is within our sphere of influence. The last thing this world needs right now is another cult or sect claiming nonsense this or that, and we are neither!

As leader of the PAC, I am responsible for organising the newsletters, events lists and physical gatherings, and this is an enjoyable and time consuming task. If you decide to run a local PAC then you can either do it yourself and interdepend or not with us ... as is your need, or, utilise the central PAC for the newsletters and mailing list. There are few rules, as I have already mentioned

I do suggest some kind of inspirational stimulus for each meeting. We tried beginning each meeting totally dry, which also works, but some kind of direction can stimulate ideas more quickly. Here follows a typical years worth of topics which we utilised for Forest Row, East Sussex in 1995. The conclusions are included, which of course would be different each time, depending on *who, what and where* ...

January 17 ... Money
What is it and how can we best utilise this most misunderstood of agreements?
Is it easier being spiritual with a pound in your pocket?
Is money a flow?
Is it an energy?
Conclusion: Don't forget fun!

February 14 ... Developing Thought Power
How powerful is thought?
Can thought heal?
Is the mental universe an actuality which can be visited and utilised at will?
How can we best develop this power?
Conclusion: Aligning spirit, mind and body is more important!

March 7 ... Sex
Is it a harmonic of love?
Is sex a creative energy?
Should it only be utilised for procreation, or does it have recreational roles

to play in life as well?

Is sex good for you?

Conclusion: The union of Soul and Mind can also be considered a sexually creative activity.

April 11 ... Language

Can words hurt?

Are words as powerful as thought?

Should words match intention?

Will language become more telepathic as international barriers disappear?

Is humour therapeutic?

Conclusion: Intention is senior to language.

May 9 ... Honesty

Is it the panacea?

Can you be mainly honest?

What is a white lie and are they acceptable?

Who judges honesty?

Can honesty be absolute?

Conclusion: There seem to be no practical absolutes.

June 6 ... Exploring Expectations, Addictions and Attitudes

Can we free ourselves from external expectations?

What is addiction?

Does the Positive Attitude Club make any difference?

Can negative attitudes be transmuted into their positive counterparts?

Conclusion: An unusually antagonistic meeting with positive results.

July 4 ... America

Do Americans lead the way in personal development?

How can we learn from their achievements?

Has independence been a necessary precursor to interdependence?

What can we offer the Americans?

Conclusion: America's purpose is to lead the way.

August 1 ... God

What or who is it?

Where is this phenomenon?

Are we all God together?

Does organised religion still have a role in modern day society, or has it

given way to individual thought?
Conclusion: There is no religion higher than truth?

September 12 ... Give and Take
Is giving a safeguard for getting?
Does outflow equal inflow, and if so how can we benefit from this knowledge?
What is karma?
Is give and take a law of the universe?
Conclusion: The giving should be the receiving.

October 10 ... Spirit, Mind and Body
In that order?
Which is the dominant actuality?
Can they exist without each other on the physical plane, or are they a good example of interdependence?
Are bodies useless, or are they a learning process?
Conclusion: Each aspect of a human being is important, and this importance needs to be balanced. Life, Consciousness and Body Of Action, were mentioned as alternatives to the title of this evening.

November 14 ... Business Creativity
Do ethics exist in the real business world?
How can business be good for the planet?
Should we profit from one another?
Is there another modus operandi available for commerce?
Conclusion: Good business can be an art form ... there is an art to being good at business.

December 5 ... Love is The Answer?
Could we exist without love?
Does altruism describe the true meaning of the concept?
Can a spirit of philanthropy be nurtured and if so to what advantage?
Is love the answer to humanity's evolutionary challenges?
Conclusion: Love IS the answer!

These topics and the questions they have posed, are to be used for inspiration only. They should never dominate a PAC Gathering to the exclusion of spontaneous and motivational conversation. A privilege of PAC events which we should acknowledge at all times, is the unique opportunity for a diversity of people to come together for an exchange of viewpoints, hopefully advantageous to all.

I have been asked a few times, if I object to a PAC being set up with a specific theme. A Christian PAC was one suggestion; I don't have a problem with that, though I suggest that the exclusion of any viewpoint is detrimental. I like to think of the PAC as a Pantheist Organisation ... defining Pantheist as *believing in all!*

AFFIRMATION ... I CONSIDER ALL VIEWPOINTS

Twenty One Steps

Fire

You can be the god of your universe, or something lesser. You have a choice. An Advanced PAC Practitioner has made that choice and begun to explore beyond the norm and into the spiritual realms of fire. I am not suggesting that much progress has been made, but the search has been instigated.

Fire, in its many guises, is the energy of our universe; as microcosms of this vaster creation we are at liberty to utilise fire for our progress. For our purpose in The 49 Steps, I talk of fire as *general energy,* not to be confused with more specific esoteric explanations; just energy.

General energy will pull you in many different directions, and it is up to the individual to harness the power and use it for good. Just as wave and wind power can be harnessed, so can general energy. If it is not, it will still exist, but not under your control. Quadrabillions of energy units are everywhere; each time we need some we dip into the stockpile. You can be the god of hell fire or the god of heavenly fire. The exact same energy is available for quite disparate usage.

Energy used to win fights and wars is the same as that used less effectively to lose them. Even considering the atom bomb, which shuddered the second world war to an eventual halt ... it is only a different way of tapping into our energy pool.

When you are cognisant of this energy pool, you may also like to consider the pool of thought stuff we plunder each time we think. This thought matter returns to base when it is no longer being utilised, and it is for just this reason, every Advanced PAC Practitioner knows that to make something physical happen, you have to *hold* the concept in your thoughts .... cling onto that thought stuff, keep it utilised otherwise it returns to base.

Use your fire wisely ... it can burn yourself and others alike. I have had occasion to watch more than one person destroy themselves with their own energy. They plot their own downfall, and weave into every hatched plan a type of built in obsolescence which ceases to function as it blows itself up. Do not bother to use your fire in the first place if you sense this type of self destruct mechanism in yourself. Expend energy instead pinpointing your mental areas of weakness, before drawing on the fire for future ventures.

AFFIRMATION ... I USE MY ENERGY WISELY

Reflection

In esoteric parlance, the years fifteen to twenty one represent the time period human beings utilise to prepare and build the mental body which will serve them for this increasingly mental oriented world in which we all live. By twenty one years of age, the personality of a human being should be completely integrated. The following twenty one years will thus be available for the development of character or soul qualities. Correspondingly, we have discussed very loosely and sometimes poetically, the state of Advanced PAC Practitionership, which of course is exactly whatever you want it to be, but could be thought of as a platform for all that will follow.

In this real world of personal development you cannot ever ask another if you have made it to a particular plateaux in your climb towards the stars. Self cognition, the only true way forward, insists that you are the only person in a position to understand exactly where you are at. This is why we do not evaluate other PAC members' positions on the PAC ladder of personal achievement. There is no need!

If you would like to read more about The Huna, or The Secret, you may find a Max Freedom Long book called The Secret Science Behind Miracles stimulating. I do not guarantee that you will find Kahu The Kahuna between its pages, but you can if you like.

AFFIRMATIONS

I AM TOLERANT OF OTHER VIEWPOINTS ... I PLEDGE MYSELF TO MY SUCCESS ... I EXPLORE MY POTENTIAL ... MY AFFIRMATIONS WORK WELL FOR ME ... I KNOW MY STORY ... I CONSIDER ALL VIEWPOINTS ... I USE MY ENERGY WISELY

Until he extends the circle of his compassion to all living things, he will not himself find peace ... *Albert Schweitzer*

The Silent Knight

Twenty Two Steps

Crystal Day   *The Antidote*

... as stories sweep the globe, and lives come and go; first there is the dote, then follows the antidote. It is a cyclical action which permits no interruption. The dote is a feeble minded silliness of imbalanced infatuation ... the antidote is a cure. That is what we accomplished after all those years. Ladies and gentlemen, thank you for listening, thank you for coming, and above all, thank you for being!

The applause thundered around the Royal Albert Hall, full to capacity for an event which only weeks earlier would not have excited three people to attend their local village hall. Crystal Day, the sole survivor of a family who could trace their origins back to the Domesday Book, felt fulfilled. Her obligations had been met and now it was time to retire ... five years beyond state retirement age for women.

The applause continued and embarrassingly, she took the stage for one last glimpse of an admiring audience ... *thank you,* she concluded.

Unused to being such a public figure, Crystal left the stage and exited the auditorium via a public door. The press soon smelled opportunity, and before she could gather her thoughts, a bombardment of questions from all angles had begun. A gentleman from the *News of the World* pleaded with her to say no more ... he showed her a cheque book and promised the best outlet for her story. She knew that newspaper and allowed the opportunity to pass. They all stood on the steps outside the hall and chaos reigned, until Crystal decided to invite order. Quite where her strength came from, she was unsure. She knew that it was nothing to do with her brain however, because whenever she tried to think, she felt no power whatsoever; just a kind of confused meandering through memory byways and shyways. Crystal flowed through that particular thinking process and transcended it onto a level of intuition ... an area of contemplation which made everything possible.

Yet Crystal remained a housewife at heart.

Married with no biological children of her own, she had become the second wife of a Polish airman who had escaped to Britain after his first wife had been killed in the invasion of Poland by Germany at the onset of the second world war. He had escaped with his four children during that invasion, and had operated with the Polish Air Force from British soil. If this had not been the case he would not have met Crystal. He was twice her age at the time, but that was no consideration of Crystal's in those days, or in fact when they married seven years after the war ended. His children became theirs and he never asked why she decided to remain known by her maiden name.

It was an anonymous marriage ... they lived in London; he worked as a trainer in the aviation business after the war, and his meal awaited him without fail, each evening as he returned from the airfield.

The children were happy, university educated, and were now married with children of their own. Crystal was a grandmother many times over and she never forgot a birthday, a name or indeed any little relevance in connection with her grandchildren. She was indeed as perfect a grandmother, as she had been a mother, as she had been a wife.

Her husband died and a few years later whispers circulated

about Crystal. Those whispers became a full toned questioning as to who she really was. *I am me,* she always replied naively! The local newspaper discovered that she had been responsible for raising money needed by The Gay Community to begin their own newspaper.

Do you agree with homosexuality, she was frequently asked. *No,* she always replied. *Then why make money available to them?* Her only response to that question was ... *because!*

The daily papers became involved. It was discovered that Crystal flew supplies to the USSR at the height of the cold war. Natural human suspicions necessitated asking her about political sympathies. *I have none,* she responded unwaveringly, *people were hungry and I felt an urge to help.*

A radio report uncovered her involvement in helping the Palestinians educate their children during awkward times. She raised money and sent books. Some people were not pleased.

And then the television report was broadcast.

Oh yes, that television report ... how her life had changed after that ... albeit briefly. Angola, Uganda, Ethiopia, Sudan, Ireland, Afghanistan, Tibet, Iraq, and finally the former Yugoslavia. A web of intrigue, admiration and wonder was spun around Crystal. Her involvements were vast, and such a wide spectrum of philanthropy was noticed, that no journalists could quite put their fingers on exactly what Crystal was about.

There they all stood on the steps, as she tried to leave the Albert Hall. *Just tell us why,* shouted a young reporter who could have been on her first assignment. *Why?* The crowd went quiet as Crystal stopped to answer. *I will answer your question in my own way and then you will ask me no more. I have my retirement to think of ... many grandchildren to cherish and an inner world of my own which I seem to enjoy more and more as each year passes.*

She read from a prepared speech.

I was born in London during that night in the thirties, when Jewish shops were vandalised, and their windows were broken ... in Germany. I was ten years old when my Father sat me on his knee and told me a story about something which happened during the first world war. The second world war had just finished and I struggled at first to interest myself in more war tales, but then I became hooked ...

It seems that an idea was hatched in 1917, when two British officers were talking over the war and its potential repercussions. They were sitting on a hillside during a cold December evening, overlooking Palestine, on the eve of a battle, when one of them, a man of outstanding character and clairvoyance, announced that his life would soon end. He made a pact with his colleague, that during the following war, of which he foretold, from his life beyond this one he would make himself available for the furtherance of *good* ... if asked to do so via periods of silence! He died the following day.

His colleague, who was called Wellesley Tudor Pole, helped instigate what came to be known as *The Silent Minute,* during that uncertain period of second world war history connected with Dunkirk, more than twenty years later. Humanity from all corners of the planet observed this *Silent Minute,* which helped create a channel between the visible and the invisible aspects of our worlds. The concept was supported by King George VI, Winston Churchill, the war cabinet and many other church and state leaders.

I wonder if any of you here remember what I speak of?

Do those of you old enough to recall war time, remember Big Ben regaining its voice on November 10th in 1940? I was only young but have a strange recollection of this daily 9 pm *Silent Minute* being talked about by all sorts of people ... most did not know of the spiritual significance and nor was that relevant or important at the time or indeed now. When interrogated in 1945, a Nazi official admitted a widespread belief in the fact that The *Silent Minute* was our secret weapon for which they could find no counter measure, even though it is a well known fact that black magic in Nazi Germany was encouraged in the highest of places.

There were millions of people taking part in this channelling that I speak of, and some of us continued beyond the obvious war time need. Indeed many of us still observe it at 10 pm each evening to this day.

What's this got to do with your charity work? yelled an old hack rudely and ignorantly.

I'm coming to that, Crystal replied before continuing with her prepared speech, unmoved by the outburst ...

I however, began to observe longer silences, until I was frequently practicing silence for an hour at a time. During these periods I noticed an intuitive side to my nature which offered particular activities up for my consideration. Whenever this happened, after the initial few occurrences which were met with my suspicion and disbelief, I began acting on my impulses.

You see ladies and gentlemen, there are those of us who think good and those of us who perform good, but few can do both, *and do!* All I did was to follow my nose. It happened to lead me into areas of present day interest, just as it could have led me into a life long study of the Bunter Beetle. If that had of been the case, your interest in me would never have surfaced, and this Nobel Peace Prize for which I am thankful, would have belonged to someone else.

Why did you never tell anyone? the old hack shouted, oblivious to Crystal's explanation that there would be no further questions.

Why would I, was the characteristic reply, *to talk about my activities would have weakened their impact. The object was altruism and not egoism! There are millions of people all around the world going about their less than glamourous businesses, helping where they can, giving where needed, talking when words will suffice. They do not shout about it for they are wise to the power of silence ...*

What is the significance of your birthday ... and your name? asked a mystical young lady, as Crystal politely forced her way down the steps and into a black cab.

That is for you all to ponder my friends, Crystal replied as the taxi drove her away.

AFFIRMATION ... I ENJOY MY OWN COMPANY

Twenty Three Steps
                    The Air That I Breathe

Many thousands of people from all walks of life, congregate in various locations to demonstrate against some abuse or other. Sometimes it is housewives and pensioners picketing ports and thereby telling the world that they are against animal exports. It could be train drivers standing at the entrance to railways stations bringing their colleagues attention to some bone of contention within their working contracts. More abstractly, groups occasionally contact one another and engage in mutual written condemnation of some sort or another.

The first point interests me most from a personal development angle. *Stop animal exports, it's cruel,* proclaim these demonstrators. *Stop killing animals in the name of science,* shout the anti vivisectionists. *Stop using animal products to test make up,* scream the body shop type enthusiasts. *Stop eating meat,* cry the vegetarians. *It is wrong to exploit the animal kingdom,* explain the Esotericists.

I believe that our purpose in relation to the animal kingdom is the exact opposite of that which most people assign to it. I believe that it is our duty to *serve* the animal kingdom, rather than the other way around. If you believe in Evolution, then it naturally follows that we, as human beings, will evolve upwards and onwards beyond the need of this physical earth, and the next kingdom in line, which by that time will comprise of individualised spirits, is the animal kingdom.

We are their behavioural examples ... and what a dismal job we make of that responsibility most of the time. A main contributing factor to this display of human irreverence for other evolving life, is that we are still capable of gross cruelty amongst our own kingdom.

From a sample, of perhaps demonstrators against the cruel transportation of animals elsewhere for slaughter, 50% of those taking part would have allowed their male babies to be circumcised. No health issue would have been part of that decision, just tradition, religion or outside pressure from others even more ignorant of the process this helpless little baby will have to endure at the hands of his elders.

There is no general reason whatsoever, for a healthy male baby to have the foreskin of his penis removed ... you think the baby knows nothing about it? Watch one having it done! Man, they are scared beyond comprehension; they frequently scream out a cry understood to mean that they are stressed; an anaesthetic is not usually administered; the operation is often performed by medically unqualified people; it can lead to infection of an otherwise healthy body part; most importantly, it can cause irregularities of the penis when that baby becomes an adult.

Why is nothing being done to stop these acts of barbarism? Well, it isn't as easy a subject to identify with as animal cruelty, even though it is closer to home. Many people who are against it, have already had it done to themselves. They like to keep the peace with their families and so succumb to pressure and maintain tradition. We still do not readily talk about those *down below* areas in public, because of embarrassment.

Personal development teachers will not talk about the subject for fear of alienating half of their clientele. They say that it is a medical issue rather than a subject to be dealt with from a mental point of view. Not so! It is a proven fact that harrowing little incidents in the life of young babies can cause lasting mental effects in the adult. Information of which the baby is not necessarily consciously aware at the time, is stored in the sub conscious and used to influence thinking patterns in the adult.

Often, circumcision is the first experience a baby has after birth, which is itself a trying time for many, but the circumcision which follows is undeclared cruelty inflicted upon the helpless baby by a sentient human adult capable of making a choice. Why chose to be barbaric? Or, if you do choose the cruel route, why not whip out a kidney, the spleen, some adenoids, the tonsils and appendix while the child is available ... it seems many of us can live without these body parts too.

As the Iraqis develop new, quicker and more efficient methods to amputate the fingers off their thieves, who may be guilty, we use the same old methods for chopping off the healthy foreskins of our young boys *who are wholly innocent.* Well, correct me if I am going astray, but that does not strike me as ethical! May we retain the right to criticise third world regimes for their acts of barbarism? *Let's get our own house in order,* is an appropriate saying to correct this criminal behaviour we have overlooked, which is occurring in our own back yards.

If we must insist on perfection, let us begin with ourselves!

It is well known that circumcision is a major part of Jewish tradition and I have no wish to upset anyone in particular on this issue. It is not only a Jewish issue however, as the vast majority of American males are also circumcised, along with many masculine millions from other faiths and nationalities.

Do not take offense! Think about it! Ponder the issue! Talk about it openly! Question the validity of this operation! But above all get real about it and stop circumcising! Just in case you are wondering if I have any particularly personal axe to grind on this subject, let me tell you that I am not circumcised and I am thankful for that mercy! I have a healthy and normal sex life and my penis and its foreskin are doing just fine thank you.

I believe in stopping cruelty to animals ... I also believe in self examination into affairs which affect the human kingdom, and this is an area which requires urgent attention. Female circumcision is a little more perverse I am afraid, and a lot trickier to deal with. You do not find many women talking about it as you may find men discussing personal matters in a public house ... *here Harry, are you circumcised mate ... no Dave are you?*

Over one billion females on this planet are circumcised. I mentioned that statistic briefly in my third personal development book called *Empowerment*. The operation again is performed on babies, and can be executed in a number of different variations. The clitoris can be cut off ... this is usually final and cannot always be reversed. The vagina can be sewn up to make the orifice smaller ... this frequently leads to extremely painful sex when such an unfortunate baby becomes adult. The clitoris can be concealed behind skin sewn over it, or mixtures of all variations including some not mentioned here.

What is the purpose of female circumcision?

Cruelty!

Male domination is what honestly comes to mind! To make sex undesirable for a woman; to ensure a woman remains faithful to her husband, the pain of sex being too ghastly to contemplate having an affair; to constantly remind a woman of supposed male supremacy and also just downright perversion. So what are all of these one billion women doing, to ensure that this mutilation ceases. Nothing! Most do nothing about it whatsoever. Many encourage it and this leads to a kind of vicious circle ... an appropriate term!

It must be said that education will lead to a quantum drop in this statistic, but it is by no means *just* the uninformed masses of the third world who succumb to this torture. Harley Street surgeries in London do brisk business in undoing, where possible, these operations, although it does seem that many of their clients are indeed of African or Middle Eastern origin.

Let's get talking on this subject ... make it okay for women to admit they have been abused in this way ... it will be easier for most to understand that female circumcision is a criminal act than it will be for much of humanity to accept that male circumcision is just baby mutilation! Stop the vicious circle.

You know, it is *not* possible to really improve any aspect of your life, whilst you continue to commit immoral acts of perhaps quite unrelated fibre. Ignorance is no protector in this physical universe. We each have to own up to all shortcomings before accelerated growth can occur of a personal development nature. You cannot commit physical crime *and* expect mental improvement. You cannot have poor thoughts *and* contemplate spiritual upliftment. All departments of your life must be heading in the same direction, and I again remind you, that choice of direction must be made at each junction we contemplate.

Real personal growth is not easy ... a few steps on the way can be ... the odd leap forward is encouraging, but the quantum leaps up the ladder are usually preceded by much thought and action of the right type.

Right thought ... right speech ... right action ... right relations ... right everything!

The 14th Dalai Lama wrote ...
True happiness springs from a feeling of inner peace and inner calm; the prerequisites are selflessness, love and compassion, and the elimination of ignorance, selfishness, and greed.

We have discussed circumcision but the subject could have been any of many. Humanity is sometimes reprehensible when judging others guilty whilst privately doing worse themselves. Sometimes, all we need is the air that we breathe. Let us keep it clean and pure. To live a vibrant life of fulfillment, a few apparently incompatible ingredients *are* necessary. Doing right in *all* departments of life is essential. TTM, silence and solitude, ascetic ability and restraint are also helpful exercises which will accelerate the growth of more outward manifestations in your personal development.

AFFIRMATION ... I BELIEVE IN RIGHTNESS

Twenty Four Steps
Who Do You Love?

The importance of self esteem is inestimable. The secret of self esteem is in knowing how to inject yourself with as much as possible of it! I'm not taking here of the *vanity type look in the mirror self worship teenage body is all* liking, although that can be a first step. I think by now you realise that we are discussing, you; the unique human being living an original story or not ... as the case may be.

You have to like yourself before you can expect others to like you. That includes *the good the bad and the ugly!* Who you are capable of liking depends on the degree of self worth you place on yourself. I suggest that you decide what you are worth, double it, and then aspire towards it.

We have to be careful not to create something artificial here. The PAC was frequently attended by a person who had previously undergone, or perhaps endured, self assertion classes, and that is what this person constantly demonstrated ... self assertion. It was hard to be around because this needless and constant self assertion was compounded by a kind of identity substitution, where another viewpoint seemed to overtake the personal one, which would have been so much more interesting.

This identity substitution was easy to spot; every time this person was asked a question, the other viewpoint was sought by her, which caused a communication lag in the answer, as the data was fed through this person's idea of what the supposed superior viewpoint would think.

Some people seem to adopt other viewpoints to the degree that they almost become the other person. It can happen, if you have been defeated by another, if you aspire towards some attributes visible in another, or if you are generally suppressed by another. To further complicate this issue, it seems that moments of pain experienced in early life, when mixed with suggestion, which the sub conscious mind interprets literally, can have a definite adverse affect on later life.

The sub conscious does not intend for this to happen ... its survival mechanism, and of course one which we capitalise on when inculcating ourselves with positive affirmations, does not allow for poetry, irony or satire ... actually, as I have already mentioned, it only tolerates literal translation, and in that it excels!

Operations are an obvious point of contemplation here, because they usually contain pain, fear and uncertainty. As with hypnotism, the patient's consciousness is subdued; in the case of an operation usually by a general anaesthetic, and when this has been accomplished, the operation begins. The subconscious faithfully records all that occurs with full perception. The retrieval of this data after the event is simple; although the full perception available at the recording stage is invariably diluted during playback.

What kind of suggestions can be available during these times ... *he'll never be the same again ... this left knee is really weak ... he said not to talk through this operation but he doesn't know what he is talking about ... I'm tired ... I love sewing ... I have a bad head.*

Notice that even communications not intended for the patients can have devastating effects on their futures; the surgeon talking about his love life ... this information can end up as a personal affirmation for the patient. We need not delve too deeply into this aspect of human behaviour in this book, but it is wise to be aware of any negative potential in our positive drive for success.

Most personal development books contain information about affirmations, but few if any discuss the negative aspects of this mechanism which really can be the rocket fuel powering your conspiracy, or the dead weight which always seems to hold you back. Now, I am not suggesting that we should all walk around for the next ten years, introverting on incidents which may contain adverse suggestions. It is entirely possible for an individual to relax into TTM and become aware of just about anything, and very definitely incidents from their own personal past track. On occasions it may be necessary to delve a little deeper into the past for relief from negative suggestion, but any advice on possibilities is outside the scope of this book.

So, we are becoming aware of negative aspects inherent in the tools we normally utilise for their positive attributes. Here is some brief advice while this subject is on the agenda ... *request silence during medical operations ... consider a quiet, drug free birth if children are about to become part of your life; drugs can help fixate negative suggestion into the subconscious .... be aware of literal comments during periods when you are feeling less than resourceful ... do not allow yourself to be hypnotised ... respect less than resourceful states in others with silence or carefully worded communication ... note your reactions to anything if they are inconsistent with the norm ... be yourself!*

So, constant self assertion was compounded by identity substitution in the example that I have used. Self assertion has little to do with self esteem and is far less important! Who you love is important, and in keeping with the following poem ...

THE SUNMAN SHINES ON ALL ALIKE
HE DOESN'T SAY WHO'S WRONG OR RIGHT
HE JUST KEEPS SENDING OUT HIS WARMTH
WITH SMILES AND KINDNESS, HOPE AND LIGHT

... I believe that it is important to love whoever you can, as much as you can, whenever you can. Begin by liking yourself, progress to loving yourself and then cruise into loving others. It isn't easy ... likes and dislikes, value judgements and incriminating stories can all lead you astray into believing that dislike is the relevant emotion to display, yet dislike is a personality type ridge and love is a character type flow.

We are dealing here in long term commitment and it does not matter that you struggle to find enough love in you to transmit to others. What is important is that you are cognisant of potential; you will then find that love will slip into your everyday life whenever it can, and the amount of it that you are able to flow to others will be in direct ratio to your real personal development.

A conspiracy for personal success is an outflow of goodness!

AFFIRMATION ... I LOVE OTHERS

Working Class Hero

What is a Silent Knight?

A Silent Knight contributed to my book called Empowerment, in an advanced way which I felt had many lesser applications. I don't mean this patronisingly, for it is aimed at myself also. Of course it is a play on words, and defines *a person who silently and anonymously flows the qualities of Love and Forgiveness into the world using thought.*

This seems to be an ultimate in altruistic philanthropy ... working unselfishly in the mental universe whilst in physical incarnation. The implications of such action are stimulating indeed. Outflow equals inflow and what you put out has to come back. If you believe that before the beginning is a thought, then good thoughts about others would naturally precede good thoughts by others about you. As thought is the creative force behind all physical universe manifestation, it seems that this Silent Knight philosophy, which at first glance may seem inappropriate, is the most relevant point we have so far discussed in these 49 steps.

By now, if you are getting into action with this book, you will have not only experienced TTM, but you will also have begun to utilise it as a tool to gain access to your inner world of mind. This personal universe of yours is part of the universal subconscious or the Akasa, which in the Sanskrit language means *brilliant, shining and, or, luminous.* It is Nature's Memory, Space, The Ether Waves and the Akashic Records. Whatever you think and mentally create, is available for perception by any other being with the necessary ability to tune in.

Telepathy is a two way phenomenon ... you are capable of both transmitting and receiving information. The mental universe is more real than this concrete solidity we view daily with our eyes.

It is also physical, but built from a much finer ether. Thought stuff from the great thought stuff reservoir, is utilised for creation in mental matter. It follows that as we are able to pollute this planet with smog, oil leaks and waste, so are we able to pollute this mental universe with low grade thoughts of staleness, hate, destruction, lust, take and greed.

A Silent Knight is the antidote to this pollution. The flowing of love and forgiveness into the astral smog surrounding this planet, which some believe responsible for the delay in Aquarian Age attributes becoming more readily accessible by a greater number of the earth's populace, is a passport into the realms inhabited by the most personally developed beings this universe has ever produced. A working class hero *was* something to be, but a Silent Knight is now more relevant for this rapidly advancing new age in which we find ourselves living and being. There is room at the top and an open invitation is extended to all who see the need for more love and forgiveness in this world.

Crystal Day is a Silent Knight, but you would never have known from the story which leads this level. She was also physically active as a devoted helper of under privileged humanity ... this affirmative action became visible and the world acknowledged her with the Nobel Peace Prize. We are many hundreds of thousands of years *before* such outcomes from mental universe activities will be apparent, if ever.

Anonymity is such a key work in outflowing goodness that it can put many people off doing it. There is no immediate physical glory like there is when you win wars or find cures for virulent infection. It is silent activity. Crystal was also silent about her physical work, which increased interest when it finally came to light exactly what she was involved with. Her goodness may have gone undetected and this would have made it even more powerful in its effects. If you are playing for the praise, the action in question becomes such a weak harmonic of its potential, that you really must consider the implications of anonymity and silence.

During your next TTM, and after you have accomplished whatever you set out to achieve, think about love and forgiveness. You can do this in a variety of ways. Remember the three different ways of communicating ... visual, auditory and kinaesthetic ... you can use the same methods mentally. Eventually you may contemplate the communication of conceptually flowed thought perhaps in the shape of symbols, music or colour.

For now we can concentrate on thought in a similar manner to the way we think about physical things. Love can be a fluffy pink ball or a breeze of pure air ... forgiveness can be a handshake or a picture of an understanding smile; you will conclude the best mediums and content for your own transmissions.

AFFIRMATION ... I AM A SILENT WORKER

Twenty Six Steps
                    Neanderthal Man

I had a Chemistry teacher who irritatingly used to constantly compare us pupils as inferior to cavemen. Quite unfairly I thought at the time, and I still believe cynically ... but it did start me thinking. That was way back in the 1960's. At the same time our Woodwork teacher taught me lessons I still use to this day, and rarely in connection with the initial subject for which they were intended. I listened to the owner of the newsagents I delivered papers for and learned effective salutations. The Milkman I helped showed me friendship. My English teacher brought the beauty of words to my attention.

My Physics teacher was unkind and this behaviour helped dissuade me from continuing to study her subject. The Religious Education teacher only lectured us on Jesus Christ, and I always felt that this was *christian indoctrination* rather than a broad view

114

of what was on offer. The Headmaster saw only long hair on me, and not what was evolving beneath it. The History teacher had immaculate fingernails and this made us take more than a passing interest in our own fingernails. Tynemouth High School was thought of as the best our area could offer in education and this made many of us feel quite special.

So many accurate and conscious recollections of all those years ago, beneath which lurk many more subconscious memories awaiting evocation. Just as humanity has evolved through many stages, many of which required help from whatever you call your particular description of Divinity, so does a human being evolve to a lesser degree through each incarnation ... endured or enjoyed ... the choice still remains.

Just as pain and unconsciousness find us at our most vulnerable from a negative suggestion point of view, so does childhood place a future adult in a susceptible position. We can take advantage of that, as do paedophiles, child employment exploiters, religious extremists and Victorian chimney sweeps, or we can respect the potential in each individual by real education.

Educo is a Latin word meaning to learn from within, and this is from where our word education has evolved, during which time we have bent the meaning somewhat to mean learning in general, and training, very much in connection with knowledge. Now, knowledge and wisdom do not go hand in hand forever and ever amen. They can exist without each other to varying degrees, and of course if you are thinking ahead of what you read here, you may realise that I am just about to uncover the real purpose of schooling, and it is of course to encourage an individual to reveal the story within. That is real education ... learning from within ... uncovering the story as the basic prerequisite to all which will follow in a successful life.

Once we understand the story, and only then, can we

accumulate the relevant knowledge for that life to be happy and successful. Some lives will require more knowledge than others ... some will require very little data and be equally valuable to society as will be those who have inculcated fact after fact into their very beingness.

Every move we make is considered by those younger than ourselves. Much of humanity does indeed still behave like cave people ... we still have cannibals on the planet; warmongers continue to attain positions of physical power; murderers prowl; molesters molest; politicians allow needless nuclear explosions. These illustrations are obvious, but we can continue with less sensational examples ... adults smoke in front of children; we fight; we criticise; we get drunk; we poke fun ... but most importantly we ram our viewpoints down the throats of susceptible children who trust us implicitly to help them into adulthood.

My personal opinion is that we educate very badly. Most teachers relate facts to their pupils and rarely have creative time to spend with individuals. When they do, then the individual is at the mercy of that teacher's viewpoint, which is more than likely the product of a fact inculcation type education. It will take many years to change our priorities in education, but that change will have to occur for us to accelerate *individual story potential* progress in a positive fashion.

Behaving like neanderthals is not just about grouping together and chanting racial obscenities from a football terrace; backward behaviour is visible whenever we fail to live up to our potential. Great lives are not created by the media, they are lived anonymously by individuals *being* their stories. We can help evolution by watching for a child's story and allowing it to unfold. Never evaluate by telling children what you think their personal story is ... childhood is a fragile time of suggestibility ... it is easy to change a young person's mind and it is also a moral crime to suppress whatever is within from manifesting in all its splendour.

AFFIRMATION ... I ENCOURAGE STORY UNFOLDMENT IN OTHERS

Twenty Seven Steps
My Way

Education is not bad!

Please do not misunderstand my observations and suggestions so far in this book, by thinking that they are all black and white, up and down, back and forth or good and bad. Knowledge of all shapes and colours has helped enormously with our forward momentum. We learned how to mass produce food and now many of us feel a need to pay a little more for our meals and eat organically produced products which have been grown small scale. This does not detract from mass production; it just illustrates that once you can accomplish something you no longer have to!

We *can* feed the world, it is just that we cannot distribute the food efficiently where it is needed, for many reasons. This mass production of food analogy is efficient for illustrating potential in education. We can, so do we still have to? By law yes, but change is in the air. There are many different ways leading to the great university of the inner world of mind, and the factual one has passed through the front door, travelled through the assembly hall and continued out through the back door where it now becomes a huge concrete square ... a little like Tianemen Square in Beijing China. It has gone beyond a good point, to rest and assess the journey it has undertaken so far.

Many byways still meander around the university grounds, some eventually lead to the front door and many don't. We need paragons in this world of aspiration, and the likes of Crystal Day have to be those which we look up to and respect. A personal story is nothing to do with the media, the lottery, the glossy magazine, the hairdo, the make up, the clothes or indeed the education.

I only placed my attention on this subject relatively recently, when an acquaintance's son graduated from Cambridge University in England. I congratulated this person and asked what his son would now do ... *he doesn't know,* was the answer. *Why did he go to Cambridge then?* I further enquired ... *I don't know! was the response.*

This graduate knew very little about anything, it transpired, and he certainly had not been helped by his father in the choice of futures available. He was meek, unworldly, easily hoodwinked, stony broke and unfortunately for him as a young adult, not very pleasant to the eye. He had studied Socrates, Plato and Aristotle during a four year course and could relate fact after fact concerning ancient history and philosophical conclusion, but the sad thing was that no personal cognitions had been realised about his own story, even though he had been in the vicinity of all this *cognisable* material.

There is more to this education lark than meets the eye.

There is my way, your way, the other way, and much to be gained from all three ways. No shames, blames or regrets need be attributed to all that has gone before ... in fact if we had not become so materialistic since the Industrial Revolution, the personal development discussion taking place here in this book today may not have been possible.

Many people have come along the trail to help humanity on its way, and one of the best loved books I ever had the good fortune to encounter was the James Allen classic *As A Man Thinketh.* This is indeed a *classic* work, which tackles a subject more contemporary now than the day it was written. The poetic flow which James Allen utilised to transmit data about the mental universe, allows ease of assimilation for a wide diversity of human types.

My particular leaning in personal development, is towards the artistic presentation of data, which ordinarily could prove difficult to both understand and practically digest into a modus operandi for successful living. This author and poet James Allen, accomplishes factual transmission in few words, compared to the amount an average manual may use in relating the exact same information.

In line with my own views on real personal development, and these 49 steps, I feel the magic of this volume lies in self cognition ... *that sudden dawning of new reality after reading inspirational words!* It happened for me with both *As A Man Thinketh* and many other books of similar sentiment, and the power of this cognitive initiation into new horizons is the most powerful form of onward progress any of us can expect from this physical existence.

To illustrate the context in which James Allen's work was conceived, we should understand a little of what was happening towards the end of nineteenth century England and in the rest of industrialised society. Materialism was rampant, and a departure from all things spiritual was the fashion for the majority of impressionable people.

Throughout history, there have always been those who were able to resist trends and retain integrity. Amongst these ranks were ever to be found the inspired and advanced members of each race. The role of a small number thus described, was to impart relevant wisdom for the furtherance of divine evolution.

In 1875, The Theosophical Society was founded in New York, inspired chiefly by a lady called Helena Petrovna Blavatsky. Theosophy is a compound Greek word formed from *theos* ... a Divine Being, and *sophia* ... which means wisdom; hence **Divine Wisdom!** Madame Blavatsky, as she is most widely known, wrote two major works amongst many others; the first, called *Isis*

Unveiled, was published in 1877 and the other, called *The Secret Doctrine,* followed in 1888.

Information imparted by these works changed the lives of many who immediately grasped a sentiment of divine history which was innately known to exist within them. Thomas Edison, one of the greatest inventors of all time, became a member of the Society, perhaps realising through it his belief in *things not seen.* He in turn motivated Napoleon Hill who wrote ... *what the mind of man can conceive and believe, the mind of man can achieve* ... and popularised it in his best known book published in the 1930's, *Think and Grow Rich,* which I have already mentioned.

James Allen was undoubtedly inspired by the divine vibrations of the time in which he lived, and this will be evident in the book if you read it. The mental universe is a plane which can be contacted with greater ease as we advance onward into the Aquarian Age, and this work can be appreciated by far more people now than when it was first published around the turn of the twentieth century.

Henry Thomas Hamblin was an admirer of James Allen, and mentions him in the book *Dynamic Thought,* which is itself essential reading for those of us engaged in progress instigated from within. Both of these authors were inspiration for the growing number of writers and researchers who began to embrace what came to be known as the Human Potential Movement of the middle twentieth century. I have already mentioned Napoleon Hill, and now include W Clement Stone, Claude M Bristol, Harold Sherman, Dale Carnegie, Maxwell Maltz, Viktor E Frankl and many more.

And nearer to present time, as well as myself, we have Brian Tracy, Wayne Dyer, Shad Helmstetter, Shakti Gawain, Stephen Covey and perhaps the man most responsible for modern interest in James Allen's work, Anthony Robbins, who regularly recommends this particular book at many of his seminars.

I mention these popular authors for reference and recommendation for some aspects of your own development, but at all times I maintain special mention for the greatest inspirers used by us all ... H P Blavatsky, Annie Besant, C W Leadbeater, Alice A Bailey, Max Heindel, the great books and prophets of many religions, and in pride of place ... you ... the individual student ... for nowhere is personal development more readily available than from within yourself!

Educo ... learning from within and developing intuition ... that is my way.

AFFIRMATION ... I BELIEVE IN MY WAY

Twenty Eight Steps
                    Sunny Afternoon

This Silent Knight philosophy came about through a combination of circumstance and altruistic intent. My friend, who calls himself *a* Silent Knight, stayed with me in England on his way to revisit a part of Spain in which he used to live. Having lived away from the language for so long, and being obliged to stay for a certain length of time, he found it a strain to be around Spanish speaking people for too long, and therefore found himself spending more and more time alone.

He was already cognisant of meditation, and supported me in my proclamations about the benefits of TTM in *You Can Always Get What You Want,* so he naturally drifted into these pastimes of inner communication, for longer periods of time than may otherwise have been the case. The weather was glorious, as it can be in a Spanish summer, so he sometimes found entire sunny afternoons drifting by as he TTM*ed* his stay away. TTM wafted into meditation, which after a while became less purposeful than it could be. He decided to think love and forgiveness into the mental world, much as charity workers do in a physical sense on the material plane.

The results are evident in his letter to me which was published in *Empowerment.*

There are many other ways of developing, and the SK philosophy, which became part of HIStory, is not necessarily part of YOURStory. We each must find our own way of service, but this I will emphasise ... *unless you outflow goodness in some way shape or form, you will only develop the faintest of harmonics available to you in this world of self improvement.*

There is a time for lazing around on your sunny afternoons, but it is nothing to do with laziness. It is rest ... recuperation ... a time for *sharpening the saw,* as Dr Stephen Covey so cleverly puts it. Preparing the tools for what awaits you just around the corner.

Angst occurs in dilettantes ... there are those who know, and those who don't know, but unless you are one of those who don't know they don't know, you better get cracking on your future. Preparation is the key to smooth success, and those sunny afternoons when you could go to the pub, eat for hours on end, chat about nothing to nobody and waste an opportunity away, are the ideal start points for conceiving of new plans, smoothing out existing strategies and scrapping those which have not worked and show no promise of so doing.

There is far less data in this book than in any of its three predecessors; the purpose of it is to stimulate, not fill you so full of facts and jargon that you are unable to sleep with the weight of them.

I have a reader who writes to me regularly with quote after quote littering each page of his letters showing just how well read he is. That is his story as it currently unfolds, but I read pain between each line. The pain and pressure of having to prove yourself, when in actual fact all the universe can ever ask of its members is to be themselves. This was much easier to accomplish when less of us were incarnated into physical life in times gone by.

You knew that life was to be a certain way during the middle ages, depending on your birthright. If you were a peasant, as were most of us, there was little if any mental pressure to improve your lot, because it was less possible then than it is now. Some think a little knowledge dangerous, and I have heard it uttered in the esoteric circles in which I sometimes eavesdrop, that it is wrong to disrupt an otherwise satisfactory life with data which can alter a psyche beyond the point of no return. Yet that is what my books are written for ... so that you may never be the same again. I know the pitfalls of stimulating thought in others, without nurturing the new viewpoints they find through my stimulation, and this is where the PAC comes alive as a kind of after sales service, if you like.

I remember having my intuition tweaked into play for the very first time. It created such a burst of energy along with a burning desire to communicate with other like minded people. I found nowhere to go, nobody to write to and few sympathetic souls. They were there, but if you do not know where to look they can remain elusive.

I started the PAC for that very reason and I am happy that it continues with its role. It is rare for the telephone number to be abused; occasionally people ring up for a free threepennyworth of help and advice, but most respect the endeavour which requires the number to be made public.

I use my sunny afternoons for the PAC. Nobody can admit to Silent Knight activities as this automatically denies them the title they describe themselves as having. Get prepared for your future. When you have finished reading this book, stop reading for a while, stop listening to others, stop mindlessly watching whatever is on the television, stop listening to music, stop criticising, stop hating, stop irrelevancies ... for a while.

Start, listening to yourself, making your own music composed in your inner world of mind, watching yourself, reading your mind, loving, understanding and applying yourself ... to your story!

AFFIRMATION ... I AM PREPARED

Reflection

By the age of twenty eight, human beings should be fully responsible for themselves, and ordinarily they would have begun the process of creating vehicles for the future utilisation of presently discarnate beings. I am unaware of more relevant esoteric correspondence for the span we have just discussed, and indeed cannot think of any until the age of 49 ... you must wait until you reach the 49th step before finding out ... so do not look now!

Stories are what this universe is comprised of. There is nothing but stories. You are a story, the planet is a story, the solar system is a story, the sun is a story ... we are part of other stories as other stories are part of ours. It is what we do with our stories that becomes life and news and HIStory and YOURStory and time and space and all that can be seen and not seen. Animal Farm is a story written by George Orwell; what a wonderful gift of analogy Orwell had, utilising it to its fullest extent in this story of the animals taking over the farm, which we can liken to what happened in Russia through the revolution of 1917.

This world is indeed a wonderful place full of ponderables and imponderables, visibles and invisibles, shinings and not shinings. We can all make our little stories fit into the bigger ones through interdependence, and acknowledgement that for every microcosm there has to be a macrocosm ... that is the law. It is not a statute made by man in a parliament or court room; it is a law of the universe ... the *uni - verse* ... the *one - song,* as Wayne Dyer describes it so poetically.

We all live the one life as individual stories ...

AFFIRMATIONS

I ENJOY MY OWN COMPANY ... I BELIEVE IN RIGHTNESS ... I LOVE OTHERS ... I AM A SILENT WORKER ... I ENCOURAGE STORY UNFOLDMENT IN OTHERS ... I BELIEVE IN MY WAY ... I AM PREPARED

A single candle can light a cave that has been in darkness for a billion years ... *Nichiren*

The Buddha

Twenty Nine Steps

Outside The Inside *Two Ways Of Escape*

I had loved the girl who called herself KT. There was no doubt about that; my feelings were neither lustful nor transient, and the passage of time since her death had not changed this situation one little bit. As I now relate the contents of these audio tapes to you, it sickens me to think of the pain she endured during those fateful last hours of her bright life.

The Stasi, a collective name for a group of individuals responsible for mass suppression of potential in around 16,000,000 Germans living east of that thoughtless line separating two distinct, yet not so distinct philosophies for around 45 years, had recorded the evidence now available for public scrutiny, that would damn them forever. *I* do not damn them, for KT would not have wished that ... they will punish themselves ... that is what KT would have believed, and who are we to doubt her wisdom.

The tablet you have swallowed my dear, will not kill you; that would not benefit our purpose, said S3 the interrogator, you will feel acute stomach pains, and I am afraid eating will never be quite the same for you. That is why it is best to tell us all we need to know.

I met KT in 1982. I was producing the recording of two songs in Minden, West Germany, and for once the project was finished ahead of schedule. I had just purchased a new Audi 80 car and had therefore decided to drive the 1,000 mile round trip. Ordinarily, I would have flown to Hanover, but I had just read the story of a family's escape over the Iron Curtain in a hot air balloon, and frankly I was fascinated. I had always wished to visit Berlin since being a child and hearing snippets on the news about Checkpoint Charlie and the Russians. Memories of that little black and white TV set seemed to somehow glamourise what must have indeed been dark times for the world. I intended to visit Berlin regardless of the time restraints of my busy schedule.

It was midsummer, as I drove along the corridor through East Germany in my flip flops and running shorts. I left my suitcase in Minden, as I would return there before driving onwards to Dunkirk, and collect it then. I believed in travelling light, but I had not estimated quite how far Berlin was. Although I had departed early in the morning for the day trip, it was now tea time, so I knew that I would have to spend the night there as there was no chance of an alert drive back to Minden.

I was stopped before entering West Berlin at Checkpoint Bravo, by a rude and ignorant border guard, commonly known as *a Grepo,* who demanded 100 Deutsche Marks for an alleged violation of the excruciatingly and deliberately painful 60 kilometres per hour speed limit. He pushed a gun through the open car window; I was scared, but that emotion was only visible if he had noticed me swallowing unusually hard and much more often than normal.

I did not acknowledge his uncouth farewell to a foreigner, and after five minutes *stand off,* he waved me on empty handed as he spat on the ground. I remembered the newsreel footage of the Americans and Russians facing their tanks towards each other during those bitter days of the cold war ... *I had just endured a microcosm of the macrocosm,* I thought to myself.

I drove directly to the Stadtmitte, passed the Reichstag, turned left into Friedrichstrasse, then swiftly turned left again into the car park, which lay behind the army huts which were Checkpoint Charlie. The high observation tower to the east, overlooked my every move, *I felt*. Opposite, there was a museum called *The Haus am Checkpoint Charlie;* I entered, and right in front of me was the balloon from the story I had just read back in England. All kinds of contraptions were on display and all had been utilised to make successful escapes from the East. The film of Peter Fechter's unsuccessful attempt was also showing in the museum's small cinema, along with happier footage of the daring dashes which were possible at the beginning of the Wall's life, but not so now that it was *impenetrable.*

What a strange place this is, I remarked out aloud.

I left and walked over to the army huts once again, and spoke to the squaddie who manned this most famous of crossing points. He said that if I converted 25 Deutsche Marks into 25 East Marks, I could get a day visa from the Grepos, which would allow me to stay in East Berlin until midnight. The official exchange was 1:1 ... the real exchange was closer to 6 east for 1 west. The Grepo at Checkpoint Bravo would have celebrated if I had paid him the West Marks he had demanded earlier in this story.

Armed with my 25 Ost Marks and still wearing my shorts and flip flops, I strode up Unter Den Linden before stopping at the Opera House. There was a ballet just about to begin. I couldn't resist it and purchased a ticket for 6 Marks, drank a half litre of Berliner Pils, and took my seat.

You know I will never tell you anything, said KT between sobs of pain, *I knew you were coming; I deliberately allowed you to catch me so that my brother could escape. He will be through the wall by now on his forged passport, and I am glad to have been of service.*

Who is this man you spend so much time with ... the Englishman

... the capitalist wimp ... who is he? the interrogator demanded to know. There was silence.

I was ashamed. Everyone wore evening dress, and there was I, the uncouth rich uncle from the west, shaming their enjoyment by showing no respect for a simple dress code. I was embarrassed. The beautiful girl who sat next to me understood. She could tell that I had been guilty only of a moment's thoughtlessness. That was my introduction to KT.

I marvelled at the one hundred strong cast of the Russian Ballet accompanied by the one hundred and twenty piece orchestra. To KT it was expected; I thought of the cost and the near impossibility of creating such a spectacle in London at an affordable price.

Don't you realise that I will never tell you what you wish to hear, continued KT, with a voice that trembled.

You sit there half naked, with a stomach burning away, and continue to defy me, shouted S3 nervously, *I have your forged passport in front of me, you were going to meet the Englishman ... you and your brother. This is the seventeenth time we have arrested you; you have been imprisoned on six of those occasions ... when will you realise that there is no escape from your homeland?*

We had drinks in a nearby hotel later that evening; KT drank cognac and I enjoyed some more Berliner Pils. It was soon time to leave each other but we both knew that it would not be for long. A bright light had been lit and it was up to us both to nurture the flame. We kissed, cuddled and fondled each other respectfully, in a dim alleyway just off Alexanderplatz. It was 11.35 and dangerously close to the expiration of my visa. KT watched as I ran down Unter Den Linden. She could not follow; a special permit was required by East Germans if they wished to travel close to that border. I noticed the faded advertising billboards, unused and uncared for since the mid 1940s.

What a strange place this is, I once again remarked out aloud.

There are no walls in my world ... KT's voice was now barely audible ... *every day since that wall was built I have travelled west on the S Bahn to the Kurfurstendam. There I have met my Englishman and each night we have made love in his car. I have been to London and met his family. We married three years ago, and the children we are raising together you will never see.*

Not one week passed without both of us writing reams to each other. Every opportunity that showed itself was utilised for visits. Always a one way flow for obvious reasons, I would have to find my way to Berlin, but once there my efforts were always reciprocated with such an abundance of love from a child who saw no reason to be any way other than giving. We would meet, eat, sleep, laugh, love and holiday. Oh, those nights we spent together were so sweet ... those days so filled with exhilaration and freedom. We spent time in Poland, Hungary and the Soviet Union; we travelled the east together in a spirit of ironic freedom in that suppressed world of fear, and always left each other at that same spot on Unter Den Linden in East Berlin, where KT had watched me disappear on the first night we met.

The audio tape ended with confused screams, a gunshot, and men shouting out orders. It was not until three weeks ago that a strange contact was made with me by a former Grepo. He found me in London and confessed his crime. He had shot KT at the border as she ran for the wall, without any real chance of successfully getting passed it. Her brother had gone back for her and during his rescue attempt he had shot the soldier guarding the interrogation and wounded him in the leg. KT half ran and was half pulled out of that building which was not three hundred yards from the border and directly opposite the Reichstag, with the wall running between the two.

The ex Grepo gave me another cassette tape, and maybe thought that in so doing his crime was exonerated. S3 had caught up with KT as she lay dying in the mud. The sound of dogs barking madly was overpowering on the cassette. Quite why S3 still felt a need to faithfully record his fait accompli seemed perverse, but those Germans were meticulous and orders were orders, *if they were.*

Caught you! What an idiot! Caught you! shouted S3, deliriously happy at the circumstances to begin with. As he looked at the pathetic sight of that girl, his long time adversary, lying there in a pool of her own blood ... after all those years of hounding her, framing her, abusing her and frightening her ... something happened. I could tell by a mixture of the sounds I could hear, and what the ex Grepo's confession was telling me. S3 went quiet and a tear came to his eye; he took off his coat and placed it beneath KT's neck. *Why did you not co-operate? You knew we'd catch you!* He dried his eyes and cleared his throat.

Oh how little you have understood of what I have said, whispered KT, barely audible above the barking dogs who would have eaten her, *you have trapped yourself in a world made by others. That wall has only imprisoned those who allowed it to. I never did. I have been free forever ... no my friend, you have not caught me; I see by those tears in your eyes that it is I who have finally caught you.*

.....

KT died in the arms of her oppressor. Four days later the wall was destroyed and is now just a distant memory for most of us. To me it will always be a symbol of all that was against the passionate views of my dead lover, without whom the world is most definitely a sadder place. Perhaps she looks on, happy to have been of service in her own small way. She knew there were many like her, just as she knew that a butterfly flapping its wings in China can create a whirlwind in America.

The ripples, she always said, *one stone thrown into a pond can create them all!*

AFFIRMATION ... WHATEVER I THINK WILL BE ... WILL BE!

Thirty Steps
What Made Milwaukee Famous

During Walter Ulbricht's cruel and tyrannical regime in East Germany, between about 1948, and 1961 when the Berlin Wall was actually built, there were no democratic elections, so six million people *voted with their feet* by walking west. When he expressed dissatisfaction with the expectations of East Germans it was suggested that he elect a new people. In Los Angeles, on a clear day you can *sue* forever. It takes several generations of *thrift* to produce a *spendthrift*. A fool and his money are soon parted, *but how did they get together in the first place?* A friend *without* need is a friend indeed. I wish I could be half as sure of anything *as some people are of everything.* One who is borrowing money from a friend should decide which he needs the most. Only the very young die good. The only place you are guaranteed to find gratitude is in a dictionary. It ought to be great fun to watch the meek fighting over the earth after they inherit it. Idealism increases in a direct proportion to the distance from the problem. Where ignorance is bliss ... it is folly to be wise. A jury consists of twelve persons chosen to decide who has the best lawyer. Knowledge is power ... *if you know it about the right people.* When a fellow tells you *it's not the money, it's the principle* ... it's the money!

My friend *a Silent Knight,* calls the above type sayings and one liners, *spirit joggers!* They have the effect of prodding you into different lines of thought from those which you may already take. Read them again if you like, they are fun. Some appear once again in this book during Level Seven, together with a whole bunch

132

more. I believe in laughter. Humour is an acceptable quick fix of well being, and one liners can have a lasting spiritual effect, which is surprising considering their superficial apparency of being whimsical and capricious.

We all have the ability to rise above our surroundings both physically and spiritually; anything which helps us to do so without removing freewill, freedom of choice and the chance to err, must be good. What made Milwaukee famous, made a loser out of some, and attention given to the quality of what we put into our bodies, will be rewarded by an increased freedom to use the body easily as a vehicle of expression on this physical plane we see all around us.

We put information into ourselves, and one liners have the effect of light and good hearted communication. In a physical sense we can say that heavy food creates heavy bodies, metaphorically speaking. If you are in the body business, as are boxers, most sports people and generally anyone who think that they *are* their bodies, then my viewpoints on diet will be less relevant to you and perhaps not very attractive.

I have researched many varied data regarding the body's dietary requirements ... a side note about my outlook on publishing houses who merely publish what may make money for them ... I was at a meeting where I discovered that a new Adelle Davis book had just been published. I had studied her philosophy way back in 1976 and it was connected to eating the right things to reduce the chance of disease. Unfortunately she died of cancer and many of us lost interest in her work because of this. I pointed this out to the people responsible for publishing this new book by a dead author; *people still like her work,* they replied. *But she's dead, how can she have written a new book,* I asked. *It's a compilation from her past work,* was the defence. *You should make that clear on the sleeve,* I thought. Money-money-money ... *the easier the better!*

I also note that Napoleon Hill has a spate of new books on release ... much as I found his work enlightening, in context with the age in which it was written, it is far less relevant than most up to date work, even if that work has included Hill's work in its research. This guy has been dead for a number of years, and we have to remember that unless editors are dedicated and understanding, these compilation type books can end up burying the original work and its intentions. Money-money-money ... *the easier the better still!*

Returning to our topic, we find that there is in actual fact, very little agreement anywhere on the subject of how us human beings should feed these bodies to not only keep them alive, which is relatively easy, but to keep them in peak condition for the lifestyle contemplated by an individual.

Linda McCartney's frozen *so called* vegetarian dishes sometimes contain egg. That rules them out for me. Also, I try not to eat anything frozen, and certainly avoid many of the ingredients Linda has included in her recipes. I remember Paul once mentioning his introduction to vegetarianism ... on the farm in Scotland, he looked out of the window where he could see the lambs playing in the fields ... they'll soon be dead and we'll be eating them, he thought. The McCartneys make things taste and look like their meat counterparts and I have never been able to identify with that outlook. Making pasta into the shape of a turkey is better than eating turkey ... but it reminds me of substitutes, rather than the celebration of a vibrant new lifestyle through eating the right things.

Linda is one of the most well known champions of vegetarian diet, and I felt that a wasted opportunity occurred when her products were launched onto the market with massive advertising campaigns. Not so however; Paul and herself have influenced many onto the vegetarian route ... just as some will stay with the McCartney's eating regimens, so others will evolve onto others.

There will never ever be anything better than pure, wholesome, unadulterated, fresh fruit and vegetables for the human bodies we currently utilise. That is the conclusion I have reached after studying a combination of dietary regimes and spiritual outlooks, then blending my findings with personal opinion.

Food combination is the correct way to eat various different foods together without causing digestion problems, and Marilyn and Harvey Diamond's books, especially *Fit For Life II ... Living Health,* is still the best work I have ever read on the subject of eating. I encountered their first *Fit For Life* book back in the mid 1980's, and I have yet to discover a finer treatise on the subject. All of the data they use in their discussions is not new; some of us will have seen similar sentiments in books espousing the Hay diet ... but the data is infinitely more advanced than that used by Adelle Davis in her books ... *old or new!*

What made Milwaukee famous was beer, and not food or diets; it is part of the same topic however, and one which we are discussing casually, rather than a regimented approach which could feel like a lecture ...

AFFIRMATION ... I AM AWARE OF MY BODY'S NEEDS

Thirty One Steps
                    Savoy Truffle

You know that what you eat you are ... an old saying that niggled away at my sense of spiritual perspective for years! I have supported the movement away from materialism for most of my adult life, and this saying always rankled me. *We are busy DOING rather than busy BEING,* I believe. Busy-busy-busy, everyone is busy with something or other. We are so busy doing that we don't even known that we already are being. But if we don't notice we are being ... are we?

Okay, I'll stop there with the abstractions ...

People are so busy they put you on call waiting so that they can accept another more important call ... I hear answerphone messages which say that the person you are trying to contact is *too busy to come to the 'phone right now* ... sometimes people are busy with me in a meeting but they are not too busy to answer the 'phone when someone else rings; *I* have to then *not be busy* whilst I wait for the conversation, only one side of which I can hear, to finish ... people are too busy to write personal replies ... *he's a busy man* is the most overused phrase to describe someone who does not wish to talk with you ...

What is everyone so busy with?

I am not so busy and yet I rarely stop producing my story! When you ask to speak to someone who cannot come to the telephone, the secretary's excuse is never, *he's relaxing right now but you will be the third call he will return when he begins working once again.* That is not the right image. We have created a busy trap for ourselves. How could Mr Executive from British Conum and Leggit explain to Mr Bigger Executive, an inspirational Monday morning spent doing nothing *visible,* when everyone knows he should have been busy doing nothing *invisible.*

Oh boy ...busy-busy-busy is the curse of our age. All of these busy people, as often as not characters in someone else's story ... too busy to be polite ... too busy to notice you ... too busy to write ... too busy sometimes to actually be busy doing anything worthwhile because they are too busy to examine what they are busy with. As I write these words the graphics designer for all of the PeRFECT WORDS and MUSIC products has just rung to tell me the printers have not been able to run a poster which we ordered, because they have been too busy with other products. Well it certainly shows where you are in the pecking order ... I wondered why they were not too busy to run the other products because they were printing mine?

What game are these busy people playing? Since when has it not been hip to spend a little time doodling with your own story ... do you get it? People are BEING busy! That is what they are. They have made busy their story. They *are* busy. Mr and Mrs Busy and the busy kids. A fine epitaph that would make too for Mr Busy Bigger Executive of the British Conum and Leggit Busy Division responsible for Business wherever it can get busy ...

Here should lie the body of a lad called Dave, but he was much too busy to be placed in his grave.
He is looking elsewhere for a better deal; when he finds it I wonder just how he will feel.
Because he's dead ... he died hungry never reaching glory; from where he is right now he lives the same old story.
Well, well, well, at last, what is this I'm seeing? It's Dave, wishing he had spent more time BEING!

Most people are too busy to look at what they eat. I know an audio engineer friend of mine from up North lad ee bah gum, who told me all about his ulcer, and on the mixing desk beside him was a half finished can of *colafizzdrinkspecial,* next to three bags which *had* contained heavily flavoured reconstituted then fried potato ... a type of crisp. *I wonder why,* I said. *I know what you are thinking Phil,* said my friend as he saw me mentally judging his diet, *it's my own fault ... but I'm just too busy.*

Call me naive but I just do not understand the logic that tells people to crucify themselves in the name of business. Is the point of living to be busy, or to discover your story and play the part? You *still* have that choice!

The body *is* what it eats, and that is what the phrase which heads this step describes. It has eastern origins but is quite relevant for western society. If you put dead rotting and decaying matter

137

taken from an animal which is no longer, into it, then that is what you will build your body from ... the life of another. That act has karmic consequences which increase as does our awareness; every action has a reaction and I wonder what will happen if we do not accelerate our progress towards being a vegetarian humanity. We hamper the evolution of a completely separate kingdom to us every time we capriciously kill for consumption. That is not to even begin touching upon the ethical issues connected to purposeless animal products like fur coats, which we parade in front of others like they prove us to be something special.

You know that what you eat you are is not just referring to the body however, and I have now rationalised the saying into its spiritual context. If you are still eating dead animals, that act does illustrate something about you, just as does the eating of fresh fruit and vegetables by vegetarians. What it says about you depends on your outlook and that of whoever is judging you. I am not judging you so please do not wait for my sentence if you are *guilty* of either or both acts.

The conclusion of Empowerment is that BALANCE in life is the chief criteria for happiness and forward progress. Balance is not fanaticism about anything. It is just as it says ... BALANCE ... like a set of finely calibrated scales. Asking some people about their diet when they have described themselves as vegetarian, I have frequently been confronted with the fact that they eat a bit of chicken or a bit of pork or a bit of this or a bit of that or a bit of the other. They just don't eat frozen red liver taken from the half dead corpse of a Russian Fish Monkey.

I restrain myself from judgement and a correction of their nomenclature because ... WHO CARES. The *worry* of what you are eating can be more harmful to you than the rotting mess you are shovelling down your throat ever could be. When you are not being too busy, then is the time to place some attention on diet and conclude what is right for your story. You are the only one who knows. I know my writing is leaning towards the judgmental here, but it is the humour that is most important ... it is very difficult to be humourous in the absence of belief which leans one way or another.

AFFIRMATION ... I EAT WHAT IS RIGHT FOR ME

Thirty Two Steps
                    A Spoonful Of Sugar

Alcohol has its good points ... it has been around for many years now. *If alcohol disappeared from this earth, so would seventy percent of my job,* said a New York cop. In the world of metaphysical aspirants, alcohol is a sign of spiritual retardment. I once attended a very serious meeting where a speaker talked at us for a couple of hours laying out his views for all to adore. He spoke of alcohol, but corrected himself by saying that in that particular room full of spiritual people there was no need to say any more on the subject because *us spiritual people do not drink it!*

I do! I confessed with a smile on my face, but I was ignored. That was the night my friendly fistula caused me to sit at the most absurd angles ... I swear that when most people were meditating, the odd thought was contemplated about the awkward Geordie in the corner. Spiritual snobbery is a fact of life which inevitably leads to people behaving *how they think others think they should behave,* and we all know by now, that is *not* living the story! It is constantly trying to fit in with some other story. Your story does not go away just because you have not recognised it, although some may have wished mine would have disappeared at that talk!

Alcohol has the effect of speeding up the vibration rate of the human body which can lead to a degree of satisfaction and a feeling of well being. This is also what we aim for spiritually, and alcohol can be seen as a substitute for real achievement. It has been necessary over the years though, and of course, like everything, whatever is available for all, will be abused by some. I do not condone the abuse of alcohol, although I have heard it said that a binge at the right time seems to wipe the slate clean allowing us to start afresh. This is an apparency and it is up to you what altitude you afford alcohol. You can do without it, although the pressures from societal habit can make that difficult. A bottle of wine seems matter of fact with a meal yet it is mentally simple to change that consideration.

Association seems to be the single most aberrant factor in the continuance of alcohol as a social necessity. *I like a smoke with a pint* ... this association links two drugs together, making them inseparable for some. *Red wine with red meat* ... why? *After a night on the beer, I like to finish off with a whisky* ... you don't have to! *I needed a drink to calm my nerves* ... it doesn't do that really. *I can't get to sleep without a brandy* ... nonsense! *I'm a real ale person* ... so *that* is what you are being. This list could grow very long.

The state of the physical body plays a significant role in the capacity for a human being to personally develop. Over the years, standards can drop and the gradual graduation effect of sloppy habits can lead to a lessening of desire to improve one's lot. That is why personal development must treat all *aspects* of human characteristics as potentially improveable, and not just the groovy ones.

AFFIRMATION ... I HAVE A BALANCED OUTLOOK ON DIET

Thirty Three Steps
                    I Can Hear The Grass Grow

The senses are affected by diet, sleep, work, emotions and relationships.

Gautama Siddartha Buddha was born a prince in Nepal, around 563 BC. In his early life he was closeted from the real world and only realised he had been living in this protected environment one day whilst out hunting when he encountered a diseased beggar. After this incident he prised himself away from what had been home and became a wandering holy man. Seeking the answers to life's mysteries, he gathered around him a small band of followers, who disappeared after Buddha concluded that the traditional religious discipline of fasting had brought him no nearer to understanding.

He began to eat again, and eventually after many years, it is believed he found enlightenment whilst meditating beneath a Bo tree. Some say he exteriorised, or was able to separate *him the being* from *him the body;* some say that he was freed from the necessity of physical incarnation; some say a mixture of both, but whatever the belief he voluntarily renounced his ecstasy for the purpose of guiding others towards the same goal.

He died at the age of 80, and many religions sprang up to keep alive, or further, his teachings. He is generally believed to be a Divine Spirit much like Jesus Christ, or The Christ. Hercules, Hermes Trismegistus, Vyasa, Shankaracharya, Shri Krishna, are thought of in similar ways.

Of course we are all Divine Beings in various stages of development, and it is during this development that we can get ourselves wound and bound in lots of irrelevant garbage rules and regulations from days gone by and still here. Much like circumcision, which perhaps had small relevance back in the days of the Jewish desert travellers and dwellers, all rules and regulations will have grounds for their existence, but more often than not they just become tradition, with nothing to offer our cause of a bright life in this day and age.

The story of Buddha has significance in that it introduces the possibilities of living life as two distinct entities which kind of interdepend on one another. Every single actuality has two distinctly different poles of exactly the same quality. Hence, love and fear are two different harmonics of exactly the same energy. Knowing this allows you an understanding of just how easy it is to turn such dichotomic opposites into each other. This is powerful data which I have already described in other books and we need only give a transient treatment here.

The opposites in a human being are often described as the spirit and the body. In actual fact, and in line with Theosophical teachings, everything, including human bodies, is spirit in various degrees of evolution ... *the consciousness of a grain of sand needs imagination* ... and I believe this philosophy to be so.

The negative pole of a human being is thought of as the body and the positive pole is referred to as the spirit. Both are needed to achieve physical consciousness on this earth. If you are aspiring towards the finer aspects of existence then it is likely you would believe those finer points to be more spiritual than the grosser aspects of life. I believe that we all aspire to be more spiritual, even serial killers of mute mermaids, and if this is the case then what Buddha achieved with his exteriorisation must be a paragon which stimulates us towards true personal development.

I am not suggesting that you rush out and become a Buddhist. I do not. Remember what I said earlier in the book about not being an anythingelsist. We are the stories we tell, not the religions we follow. Be your story, it is the easiest thing to be, believe it or not.

It would be nice if we could all achieve this exteriorisation phenomenon though wouldn't it? I have heard stories about piano players who could sit in the auditorium whilst watching themselves playing the grand on stage. People have told me that they are capable of walking around whilst *being* a few feet behind their heads. I have listened to success stories where people described themselves as being the wind, being trees and being this that and t'other, but rarely have those on success ladders been content to be themselves ... Jim *the window cleaner* ... Joan *the shopkeeper* ... Mr and Mrs *Nothing special from a media point of view!*

The only expression of happiness I ever heard which touched me in this context, was delivered by a car panel beater who had attended a school with *theosophical leanings,* not far from where I live. He was extremely well spoken and I knew his family were financially comfortable. His private education had been paid for, he was charming, knowledgeable and the world was his oyster, so to speak. I was guilty of asking him what he really wanted to do ... he didn't understand the question and as I repeated it I realised that I had missed the point. He said that he always wanted to be a panel beater throughout his education, the manner of which had encouraged him to be creative in whatever field he chose. *I am really happy,* he said. I learnt a lesson!

I examined this school with a view to my own children's education and decided against it. There was such a singular lack of *any* type of competition inherent in all of its philosophy, that we shied off. I believe ultimately that this competition free environment has terrific potential ... especially with artistic children, but the time did not feel right for us, and we *the parents* nurture that competition free aspect of education in our children whilst sending them to regular schools.

So many choices and decisions to make!

If exteriorisation is the aspiration, then degrees of it would result in benefits also. I remember undergoing a particular course of spiritually enlightening exercises where I most definitely felt extremely light and unattached to anything negative within myself. That was a degree of exteriorisation. I sampled a separateness which led to a feeling of interdependence. Good news has a similar effect.

You may know the true story of a businessman in America who was just about losing his business in San Francisco. Avoiding bankruptcy depended on him closing a deal in Seattle, from where he called his wife just before this all important meeting. His wife listened to his moans, groans, fears and heartaches and the bad vibes from him jumped out of the receiver at her. She knew he would blow the deal with that attitude so she therefore decided to give him the good news ... *we've just won three million dollars on the lottery*, she announced, *forget the deal!*

She knew he wouldn't however, because that business was his life, and he went into the meeting feeling great, not caring whether or not the deal was clinched as it no longer financially mattered to him. The clients liked his attitude and he closed the deal before excitedly returning home.

Show me the money, he said to his wife through a broad grin. *What money,* she replied, *I invented that story of the win to make you feel better!*

AFFIRMATION ... I TELL MYSELF GOOD NEWS

Thirty Four Steps

Country House

How much of a relationship is there, between visible wealth and personal development? Probably very little, although it is impossible to prove. How often do we hear stories from winners of huge amounts of money saying that they are going to do this, that, and then more of this with it, but rarely, never in my case, do we hear anyone say that they are going to use their newly found wealth to allow them time to find themselves; evolve; look within; develop themselves ...

When you come into some money you buy your big house in the country and everything else fits into place. We all know *obviously* that it does not. For many, changed financial circumstances are the beginnings of their personal downfall. I have described in previous books, my observations of some rich and famous people whom I have worked with over the years, and I rarely noticed happiness along with the financial and social positions they found themselves in.

Why?

It is because people do not distinguish between what is outside and what is inside. That is why ugly stories of personal development through possessions are damaging to the image we should observe in this business. Owning a jet helicopter is not even a stimulus to aspiration for others! It is stating that personal development is something outside and *that* it certainly is not.

We all know numerous stories of rock and film stars at their peak, committing suicide or accidentally overdosing with drugs. Why are they using drugs in the first place, if they are at the pinnacle of their aspirations? Surely there are grounds to believe that the outward manifestation of success does not match the inner. If drugs are still necessary even when all has apparently been achieved, what hope is there for those of us who have not yet peaked? What is the point of getting there if we still need drugs once we have arrived?

Many questions, but the subject of *what is there,* once we arrive, is important if we are not to encounter disappointment after disappointment during the journey and at the terminus. BALANCE again is the issue here, and if equilibrium is not attained during the route to success, between outward and inward achievement, then the ride will be rough and the achievements questionable. Even if the balance tips in favour of inner accomplishment, problems can arise when a person's physical altitude is beneath the mental awareness.

A good old analogy can be used, if Gary Glitter doesn't mind. Gary Glitter for those who were not conscious during the seventies, or perhaps were unaware of the British rock scene then, was massively successful as a Glam Rock star. Unfortunately, his friends were Elton John and Rod Stewart, who both wrote many more songs. Elton as a co-writer mainly with Bernie Taupin, and Stewart occasionally solo, sometimes with others and often like Glitter, he sang songs written by composers other than himself. The point is that they were and are vastly richer than Glitter ever was. As they socialised together, Gary Glitter had to keep up with the Johns and Stewarts, and ended up spending more than he earned which resulted in his bankruptcy.

The most famous story of his during the seventies was when he arrived at JFK Airport in New York, and there was no limousine to collect him. He angrily returned to the UK without leaving the airport, before taking the same 'plane back to New York after ensuring his car would be there to collect him. The story is apparently true.

The analogy lies in Gary Glitter's bankruptcy, which meant that he was as famous as ever, yet totally and utterly broke. This meant that he was made to use public transport, where he endured the resultant rapport with his public, which fortunately was usually good natured. His financial position did not balance with his public persona. A ludicrous situation was the result.

This is exactly what happens when *in and out* are not balanced, although the imbalance would usually be less obvious and harder to locate. It is like training someone to perform brain surgery, training them again, then refusing them access to a patient on whom they can put that training into practice. There would be an imbalance of significance, data, or knowledge, with practice and physical experience.

Imbalances of this sort can produce sickness. There are many other types of imbalance too, but they usually reduce to, the ratio of abstract significance to physical manifestation. If you live in a house and it's a very big house in the country, then check your balance of in and out. It is quite remarkable just what a tweak and a nudge, a turn and a twiddle of the calibration knob can mean to your potential for happiness

Just where do drugs fit into your life?

AFFIRMATION ... I BALANCE MY INs AND OUTs

Thirty Five Steps
Tweeter And The Monkey Man

The above title is taken from a Bob Dylan song on the first Travelling Wilburys album. It is a loose story of two characters in the title who were hard up for cash ... so they stayed up all night selling cocaine and hash. Ever the easy way for so many people to both earn money and get high. Social drugs are not the only concern which the world of personal development extends its sphere of embrace to ... alcohol we have already mentioned ... nicotine through smoking speaks negatively against itself ... but the myriad of medical drugs prescribed and dispensed willy nilly by doctors and pharmacists the world over, are giving rise for concern.

Whilst writing this I have spoken to someone with sciatica who consulted with a doctor and was prescribed painkillers. I gently mentioned to this person, still experiencing some discomfort, that painkillers would only suppress the symptoms and would not address the cause. *Really?* was the surprised response. I wonder why the doctor failed to mention this fact to the patient. Lack of time, limited concern, the need to know basis, don't blind with science; whatever it was, there was no proposition to include the patient in any kind of cure plan. Get rid of them as quickly as possible with a prescription, a sick note, and if you are lucky, a smile. Very lucky!

Medical doctors are not *usually* very cognisant of remedies which have not been mentioned in their mainstream training, or the journals they read. They rarely have or make the time to extend their knowledge of fringe medicine or new age medical philosophy. In fact many are downright against so called quack cures. Fortunately, although I believe in many quack cures, I avoid nostrum mania and do not feel compelled to embrace the topic in too fine detail here.

What concerns me is the lack of involvement a patient gets to have in his or her own cure. We go to the doctors and kind of absolve ourselves from all further responsibility. In my early singing days I developed a very sore throat and went to my National Health doctor as a last resort to ask for help. I was brushed off with a prescription, and when I mentioned that I did not take drugs, except as a last resort, I was grudgingly and cynically assured that this particular prescription was drug free. I accepted it with suspicion and presented it to a doctor friend of mine who has a private Harley Street practice ... he told me that the prescription was drug free *except for the morphine in it!*

That particular National Health doctor, who was singularly anti anything except his own viewpoint, has now thankfully retired. I may as well let you know that I believe we are inherently capable of curing anything whatsoever that goes wrong with these physical vehicles of ours, without any external help at all. I write here of capabilities! Potential! In actual fact, few of us are able to operate the remedy as well as we effect the fault. This means that the philosophy that I espouse and write of here, is once again relegated to the position of paragon instead of existent. So, as it is an ideal scene and a fact that the human body can cure itself of anything this earth can throw at it, surely the more we involve the patients in their own cure the quicker will be the instigation of self cure into humanity's modus operandi.

Regardless of the above, it is a medical fact that patients

psychosomatically affect their own cures. If you think you are getting better ... you do! If you think you are getting worse ... you are! To get the brush off from a General Practitioner for any reason, when you ask to be involved in your own cure is downright stupid, yet I know this to be so in many cases.

You do not need regulations or Acts of Parliament to begin the instigation of self cure into your life. You do not need to change the thinking of ten thousand General Practitioners. Through gradual graduation, you can begin to instill into your own thought patterns that your mental power extends to your physical body. During TTM you can communicate with your body just as you would expect to communicate with God during Christian prayer. Any prayer is telepathic no matter what is the object of your transmission. Answers to prayers are also telepathic. All transmissions and receptions of thought are telepathic. In this thirty fifth step we are concerned with our own innate ability to communicate successfully with our physical workings.

My first introduction to self cure many years ago, is also the simplest and most effective method I have yet encountered. Uncommonly, I had a bad head. I was asked where the pain was. I described the location. I was asked what colour the pain was. In my case I replied red. I was recommended to move the pain to the right ... then to the left ... then back to the centre, before once again being asked the colour. It had changed to pink. We moved it about some more before mentally discarding it in the bin ... and I swear that is where it went! I felt much better.

You can do this yourself without the external help I had during my introduction to this potential ... but this is just one of a myriad of techniques which are available now, and still being invented. We are all capable of inventing new techniques and it is up to the individual to begin the utilisation of self cure for the human body.

Reliance on drugs is on par with the acceptance of external

manifestations as proof of your own personal development. Both are so downscale from where we should be at in this day and age. The future is about *light and love and power,* not uncertainty, reliance and weakness!

I am aware that many of my illustrations are simplistic and at times incomplete, but you know it is not only me who will be instrumental in the discovery and inculcation of new ways and outlooks into your existence ... you are the most important component in your own success story and this is *not* an instruction manual. There are loads of them on the market but they rarely if ever address the areas I am identifying and stimulating.

Too much information causes an imbalance and this incessant thirst for knowledge which becomes more apparent as each day passes, is a symptom left over from the Industrial Revolution. The less well offs discovered that they could be educated, then many became downright obsessed with it as they climbed the social ladder. Because this education was of the outward type, many inner feelings that *uneducated* people used to rely on, were relegated to a heap called superstition. Hard fact became the order of the day and we were all encouraged to strive for more of it. Some people know so many facts that they do not know themselves ... there is no time or space for such personal irrelevance.

The well offs were often so obsessed with tradition and suppressing those beneath them that they spent all of their time defending who they thought they were ... son of whatchamacallit ... daughter of Lord Howsyafather. We still do this to a lesser degree when we describe ourselves as something. *What are you? ... oh, I am a surveyor. Where are you? ... middle management.* What I ask is ... *when are you?* The answer often enough is ... *never!*

AFFIRMATION ... I AM ME

Reflection

Diet, drink, drugs, habits, new and old, good and bad, you and your friends, your friends and yourself, food combining, junk, affirmations, positive thought, negative feedback, anythingelseism ... when I reflect over what I am transmitting to you by medium of the written word, it strikes me that I am guilty of a crime which I invented; it reminds me of that excellent George Orwell book called 1984 ... I call this crime INFORMATION OBSESSION!

But *you* know that is a superficial supposition. I am not guilty of anything, although some can often make you feel guilty of just plain downright BEING! Guilt can cause more *dis*-ease than lack of information ever did, could or will. Guilty feelings in the absence of crime are actual adversaries of balance. It is well worth affirming, especially those with a religious upbringing, that real guilt about anything only exists following the injury of another by yourself. Even then it is a second rate emotion suitable only for the less responsible members of our community. Shames, blames and regrets ... that trio of suppressive cavaliers are always available for your indulgence whenever you care to call on them.

Do not ever blame yesterday ... remember that life is today. Be responsible and do not waste valuable time regretting anything. Create your tomorrows and nurture that Divine spark which is you. Always be above anything that is denser than the light being who is you. The easiest thing in the world is to create mysteries about the simplest things in life. You are nothing else but you, so if you just concentrate on being you, happiness will be forthcoming.

AFFIRMATIONS

WHATEVER I THINK WILL BE ... WILL BE! ... I AM AWARE OF MY BODY'S NEEDS ... I EAT WHAT IS RIGHT FOR ME ... I HAVE A BALANCED OUTLOOK ON DIET ... I TELL MYSELF GOOD NEWS ... I BALANCE MY INs AND OUTs ... I AM ME

... you say you want to show them heaven from where they stand! Jon, they can't see their own wing tips ... *Jonathan Livingston Seagull*

The Graduate

Thirty Six Steps

The Wayward Sheep

One day not too long ago from a cosmic standpoint, a shepherd in Leeds felt ill. Now for those of you unfamiliar with the geography of these British Isles, Leeds is beside Bradford and Bradford locates itself at the southern most extremity of that line of hills we call The Pennine Chain. This is not essential information on the face of it, and there are those reading these words right now who are thinking *get on with it!* I know that feeling so I respect it and will indeed get on with it, but only after describing the terrain in which this story has its beginnings.

The towns of this area, I know they will forgive me for describing them so, are generally grubby, and the surrounding countryside magnificent, so it does seem apparent that the population of this area are able to enjoy some degree of balance in their lives. To the west is Lancashire and to the east the vast majority of the Yorkshires. To the south one would encounter the lesser north, and to the north one would reach Scotland if not waylaid in Newcastle.

Leeds is quite a happy place, but it did not seem so when the shepherd awoke with a feeling in his head worse than that experienced when passing a square kidney stone. It seems that the amount of happiness exhibited by the populace of Leeds is in direct proportion to the amount of ale they supped the previous evening. As our shepherd friend had contributed to the image of Leeds by quaffing more than he needed not three hours prior to him awakening, he felt justified in trusting his sheep a little more than would ordinarily have been the case.

As the year was 1760, the mode of transport was horse if you were fortunate, and foot if not quite so ... that morning our friend achieved further balance by attracting the attention of an acquaintance who was travelling in the general direction he was heading, and was thus able to secure a ride. He pondered his good fortune briefly and his aching head lengthily. By sunrise, the usually persnickety shepherd was once again safely ensconced on Ilkley Moor, and for the record his hat was firmly in place.

He counted his sheep and gave thanks, as was his habit, for the flock being safely transported through the darkness of night into the life of day. However, the lasting effects of the alcohol he had imbibed only hours previous, had made him somewhat forgetful, and consequently the faithful hound who had remained with the sheep throughout the night, and who was called Maxinne, went without her usual quota of gratitude.

Max was an ugly bitch as they go, but this had not ever been the cause of undue attention from her master, who always paid more attention to the character of his Border Collies than his colleagues ever did to theirs. The misshapen nose, red coat, bushy tail and half bitten left ear which were Max's, had not been offensive to the shepherd's eye when he purchased her at the age of six weeks from the breeder, who had charged him six shillings for the privilege of ownership. When the usual question was raised as to the whereabouts of the dog who fathered Max, the usual reply of *now deceased* was accepted, and no further thoughts were harboured about the features of Max, which definitely excluded her from any dog shows only allowing thoroughbreds. Nor did the shepherd object when fellow shepherds called Max, *Foxy,* for he was singularly unaware of any questions concerning the pedigree of his loyal servant.

That day however, he noticed just how ugly Max was, as the dog plied for his attention, stimulated by the lack of earlier gratitude shown by her master. The shepherd even made his surprise audible when he patted her on the head and commented, *you are an ugly bitch aren't you!*

By midday, the shepherd noticed that his sheep had not eaten as much of Ilkley Moor as they could have done were he not hungover and able to show them greener pastures, but he knew that it was months before market and future gains would easily replace earlier losses. It was a doubly unlucky day for Max however, because on finding the number of his sheep suddenly having been depleted by one, the shepherd uncharacteristically, but relatively gently, kicked his dog up the backside and withheld her food.

The dog was unsure as to why her fortune had changed radically in the space of so few hours, but remained faithful never the less, only faintly aware that her master no longer looked at her in quite the same affectionate manner. She was ordered to find the missing sheep, and was reminded that six shillings was still owed, that sum being the initial purchase price of the bitch from the breeder.

Max ran on ahead and the master followed her. In the distance behind them both, for some reason the flock ensued. Whether they sought Max, the shepherd or the missing sheep, was unclear, but follow something they did, and it led them in the same direction as the two animals and one human.

Now, the lead sheep unwittingly left a trail behind her. This was easily followed in its own right, but given also the fact that she urinated, defecated and at one point even regurgitated some spoiled grass in her own footprints, Max was not even stretched in her task. This trail however, was more difficult for the shepherd to walk, as it had been trodden through virgin woods. Skillfully, after straying a good few miles to the west, the lead sheep headed due south*ish* for no apparent reason, trampling all that grew in her way. Faithfully, Max followed and made that trail even more definite. Grudgingly, the shepherd sporadically caught up with his dog, and spookily the whole flock followed.

Day became night twenty times over, before the shepherd laid his hands upon the lead sheep, who for the previous five nights had been accompanied by Max, who had forgotten why she was following the sheep in the first place. As the shepherd placed his hands around the sheep's neck and once more placed a gentle kick up Max's rear end for getting too friendly with the aberrant flock member, he noticed two things ... firstly a sign which read *Cricklewood,* which he would not have known was a village on the outskirts of London, as it was fully two hundred miles from Leeds; and secondly the fact that the ensuing flock had caught up with them all and were now grazing by, awaiting instructions from the shepherd, Max, or I daresay the wayward sheep.

The shepherd was fastidious, turned them all in a northerly direction and bade Max forward. Max nipped a few heals and they all got the message, blindly following whatever was in front of them without any thought resembling that of which humans are capable. Even though they forgot what that message was within seconds, they still walked on for a further twenty days and nights before they were once again breathing Yorkshire air in Leeds.

The shepherd was tired and irrational. The distance between Leeds and Ilkley Moor was his straw that broke the camels back, and he decided to walk them no further. Instead, he showed them to their owners residence who was shocked to receive the resignation of his trusty shepherd after thirty years of trouble free service, and promptly ordered his bailiff to kick the shepherd's backside regularly until it was three miles from the owners land.

The ex shepherd drowned his troubles that night in a grubby inn more famous for its filth than its ale, and recounted the story to a herdsman who sought transport for his cattle to the smoke of London. *I can give you directions to Cricklewood but not London,* said our ex shepherd ... *why, I have a sister who lives in Cricklewood not ten miles from where I am taking this herd to market,* replied the herdsman before receiving instructions.

The following night a pig farmer was blessed with the ex shepherd's directional wisdom, and the night after that a similar story was unfolded to a horse dealer. Each time the ex shepherd passed on his wisdom, he was rewarded with drink, until he became famous throughout Yorkshire as *the drunk sage in the grubby inn.* He sold this wisdom on his deathbed to the innkeeper, who sold it on to the original shepherd's son who sold it to his brother and onwards it went to his brother's son.

All the while, the trail became a track became a path became a road; all the while, more and more used this route, each following the other, and by this time all unaware that they had a wayward sheep to thank for their good fortune. Until the 1960s that is, when a civil servant noticed that this road everyone seemed to use between Leeds and London, went first to Liverpool, then to Birmingham, before arriving at Cricklewood via Coventry. This civil servant being a wise man, and only working for the government because his Father had lost the Family farm in a bet during the war, realised that this was silly, and urged the government of the day to build a more direct road, which became Britain's first motorway known as the M1.

Many years later it was noted by a writer who had been alive during the building of this first motorway, that much like the followers of that sheep, humanity makes similar mistakes in ways of the mind. Blindly following ruts in the brain, *man is prone to habitual thought rather than thinking habitually!*

AFFIRMATION ... I QUESTION MYSELF

Thirty Seven Steps

Mrs Robinson

There are so many varied ways of graduating everything, that I doubt the validity of much personal development data frequently. Until that is, I reflect on the power of stimulation, which subjectively, can sometimes be entirely unconnected with the result it produces.

The biggest single mistake anyone can make in relation to their own development, is to think that they are beneath the potential for real change. Phantom prerequisites float through minds, reminding those who succumb to such externally imposed thoughts, that real personal development is not for them because they have not as yet done *such and such this and advanced such and such that.*

I am only a housewife ... I am just a mechanic ... how many times have I heard these self imposed suppressions and patronising qualifications; just think how responsible these thoughts or negative affirmations are for reducing a persons self worth and esteem to worrying low points.

Nonsense! Tut tut nonsense!

We are all capable of quantum leaps up the PAC Ladder and beyond. It is the state of mind that counts and not the so called prerequisites. Future gains can be so out of character, that they defy belief by onlookers. Witness the letter which comprises the following four steps, from a dear friend of mine called Dan. This guy is in his eighties and recounts part of his story from memory. We all have the chance to write our stories in advance however, as we are now in possession of the inspiration that this is indeed possible.

You can compose your story before you live it; or you can write it from memory if you have lived part of it or perhaps if it was written by someone else for you. Dan agrees that the latter is what his story was to begin with ... an externally imposed expectation which became inculcated internally as if it was his own. Yet, self penned stories rarely have such unreal expectations built into them like Dan's ... as you will read.

The first method of writing one's story in advance is what this book has concerned itself with, and if that is the only cognition, or self realisation that has been forthcoming from your involvement with my work, then I am successful man!

AFFIRMATION ... I WRITE MY OWN STORY BEFORE IT HAPPENS

Thirty Eight Steps
                    Breakfast In America

5 JANUARY 1996

Dear Phil,

I have just finished reading your letter, then the floppy disk and again your letter. I have now gained more understanding of what is going on inside your universe, *and,* with your fourth book, to which I offer a synopsis of *my* story.

In my dotage, the stories acted out on this material plane of *personalities and differences* has become less and less interesting. There is a great attraction to my attention, drawing on it more and more, and insisting it becomes aware of the parallel universes ... not to know more about them through the study of second hand knowledge, which is itself a very important part of our human story as you call it, but to know *first hand,* by experiencing, through moving my attention and awareness into those realms.

This desire of course, can steer the neophyte into drug experiences to which I know you are a committed opponent, as we both know that one's only experience in indulging drugs, is the drug, that s all. Being a crutch which drugs definitely are, they do not allow us to build the strength required for prevailing to our cosmic potential.

Sounds smug of me doesn't it? Well, maybe my shingles pain could serve as an analogy here. I am now almost four months into this debilitating condition, and if I looked for improvement day by day, I could feel very discouraged. I have to look back many weeks to remember how it was then and make a comparison; and I then have to state I am very definitely better! Well my spiritual level, grade, or whatever you wish to call it, follows somewhat the same curve. I have to look back at much greater intervals however, like 5-10 years, to be able to honestly say I am spiritually a better person. It's like watching a flower or plant grow. If you try to persist looking until you see a difference, it never comes to most of us. Time lapse photography however, allows us to see the marvellous procession of an intelligent force at work, which knows exactly what to do at each step.

So I am better than before. How do I know this? Because of the inner peace that continues to grow inside of me, and the greater absence of strife and discontent. Finished? Never! Imagine anyone declaring that he or she has attained the final end state of Total Enlightenment? Perhaps by wearing a badge, or a bracelet as do some cult members, to show off their spiritual level. Better to wear a chip on the shoulder as they used to do in the old days and dare someone to knock it off! That s just the way the game is on this physical plane. On other planes, this type of one-up-man-ship does not appear to be relevant, as you say.

Eternity and Infinity make such personality evaluations non sequitur.

I feel sure my previous lives were predominantly spent in the East, because it is part of my nature to remain out of the main stream of life. I have been blessed really, to have been born into a family that showered me with goodness beyond the average. So much so, I felt, and still do feel somewhat, that I have done very little to earn all the beautiful life I enjoy. This made me rebellious in my youth. I wanted to be acclaimed for my brilliance, or my ability, or whatever, as a result of my own self direction ... ha! I found fault with the old fashioned ideas of my parents and mocked up some kind of conspiracy, in the vulgar sense of the word and not your artistic *breathing together* sense, on their part to throttle my self expression. They just weren't with it in the new science oriented age.

I therefore broke away and went to sea, and mocked up myself as a great adventurer, sailing the oceans and being the worldly tale teller of far away lands. Boy, what a fantasy! Outwardly I may have played the part well to most people, but inwardly I was running scared the whole time. Then of course, there were always a few so called mates around and about me who would challenge my brave and carefree personality by engaging me either in physical rough-housing, which I had no talent for or interest in, or testing my intellectual deductions until I felt disgracefully vanquished. This would expose the real me as being the biggest of all cowards. I would actually go off alone and cry sometimes. So much so that in most cases I would take off for another environment, completely disconnecting from the last, so I could act out the part I had chosen for myself. This involved me mainly identifying with a composite of the characters from the novels I had read at that time. Taking on another's identity as some describe it, or what you call *Identity Substitution.*

One of the most difficult things in the world to do, I think, was to be forced to admit, declare and confess before the entire universe, as it appeared that big to me at the time, that I was a liar and a fake. I really identify with those politicians, ministers, and even criminals, that are placed in a position where they cannot deny the actual evidential proof that they have been fooling everyone with what they are doing. It is disastrous! It is no wonder they behave erratically when they simply disappear, commit suicide or change names to avoid their responsibilities.

Not being prepared with another way of thinking and behaving, one is left with the desolate feeling of not only being very alone, but also with the feeling of being a non person. The very humiliating and alternate solution, is to admit to all those one has criticized as being old fashioned, wrong, stupid and mean, that they were actually the only source of real security and stability one had. That's going back to the same dependent state one was trying to get rid of. Not me, no sir; I was too proud, full of youth and energy. All I needed to be as good as anybody else was to have a degree!

It had been pointed out to me loud and clear in the Armed Services that I did not know enough, because I had no degree, to be of any value as far as opinion was concerned. Those who levelled these affirmations at me were mostly the new officers just graduated from Officers Training Academy, or OCA. I was not permitted to even apply to OCA because I had quit after my two years of college without a Degree. I didn't need that stuff! Oh boy!

Having come out of the Army with four and a half years of earned credit for college under the GI Bill, I mustered out and leaped into The University of California at Los Angeles, the famous UCLA, to get a degree in Engineering. Somehow I had great confidence amid all my neurotic feelings of inferiority, that I could be outstanding as a student. Hadn't I done so in High School ... as the only student in my class to once solve a calculus problem ... being chosen by the geometry teacher to explain certain theorems to the class they were having trouble with ... not to mention my Mother always telling me *how smart I was!* ... a valuable affirmation from her to me; and boy did I learn what a golden element in my makeup that was as I progressed in life.

My first 2 years in UCLA were a breeze, as I mainly reviewed subjects which I had only been away from for about 13 years: Analytical Geometry, Differential and Integral Calculus, Differential Equations, Mechanical Drawing, Organic Chemistry, Accounting and some others I have forgotten. I was on cloud nine as they say. I was in peak physical health because of the Army's required Calisthenics. There were about 20,000 students, and only a few thousand males! Even those were rather young, inexperienced and just out of high school. I joined a Fraternity and eventually became the treasurer. It was my fate to experience being adulated day and night by the most beautifully sexy girls on the campus, because of the scarcity of males. All I had to do was walk into any Sorority house and these adorable young things would ooze into the living room, looking me straight in the eye with their most fetching smile and a toss of their pretty heads. It was reminiscent of my army days when I would stoop to entering a house of the Easy Virtue Ladies for my carnal appetite to be satisfied.

I gorged myself with ecstatic pleasures, sometimes taking two or three girls out on the same evening. My starving male ego was satiated even beyond a point that I began to think I really was God's gift to the most gorgeous women who walked this earth! I could identify with the movie stars, some of whom I would see often in Westwood Village and Santa Monica. I could still wear my uniform and go into the Beverly Hills Country Club free of charge, where I actually played a few holes with Adolph Menjou and Clark Gable on different occasions, and my favorite pianist Hoagy Carmichael even came into the Frat house on some weekends; he was a brother and would let his hair down in our vicinity once in a while. This was the highest living I had ever experienced! I was, as it is said, *in tall cotton!*

Why do all ecstatic things have to come to an end? I did find an answer which I will hold back for a while. It was however, destined to reach its *climax* ... a very fitting word for the type of life I then led. The first blow to my delicate male ego occurred about ten months into my first year at the University; Japan had surrendered and the boys were coming home in droves. Overnight tens of thousands were entering the U ... girls who would actually call me out in the night for any little old thing I wanted them to do were politely letting me know that things were different and very busy for them now. I soon found myself with a couple of old stand -bys and had to face an awful truth: When there is a shortage of men, women change completely into aggressive, manipulating beings who use men just as men use women when they can get away with it.

This was bad enough, gads, I hope I am not boring you with this, but I shortly began my third Junior year and started studying material which was entirely new to me; I found there were actually subjects that I could not comprehend! Now of course I know that I had passed not one, but many *misunderstood words,* and noted that you discouraged this in your book *Before The Beginning is a Thought.* My basic, and only real grounds for any self confidence I might have had, was revealed to me as a fantasy. *I was not at all as smart as I had thought.*

It was at about this time that my physical condition, which had been tops, began deteriorating. I contracted headaches and acid heart-burn. I felt very nervous and began to get a feeling of terror inside me when I would go into class and the professor would announce there was to be a little ten minute quiz! Absolute terror! So bad that even though I might have known the answers, I could only watch the clock and felt sure there would not be enough time for me to answer. Consequently, many times I would turn in a blank paper or leave the room to vomit.

I was not smiling any more, and some of my fraternity brothers chided me with the observation, *well, smart-ass ... you re not so smart after all, are you?* or words to that effect. I guess I had been rubbing it into them all along ... beyond my awareness. What did I have remaining of worth? All the joy and pride I had garnered had left me desolate, lonely and ashamed of myself. Suicide was often in my thoughts. I doggedly crawled through my junior year getting Ds and Fs on subjects I could not comprehend, mainly due to my worrying about myself in a most negative manner. *pause ...*

AFFIRMATION ... I AM CONFIDENT

Thirty Nine Steps

The Thirty Nine Steps

It would not have been fitting to call this step anything but the title it has. The John Buchan book of the same name is one of the finest works of fiction describing escape, wrongful accusation, politics, intrigue and happy ending, that I have read ... *not forgetting the glorious romps through the Scottish countryside.* In fact that book has elements in it parallel to most people's lives.

continuing Dan's letter ...
At that time, there was no Senior year at the Los Angeles University of California and I had to transfer to Berkeley for the completion of my course. Being a long way from Hollywood, Los Angeles and the swinging crowd of that area, Berkeley was much more sedate and straight-laced. Anyone from UCLA was a bit frowned upon as lower in class, even though tradition forced the Fraternity to accept me as a brother. With literally a constant empty and lonely feeling in the pit of my being, I was determined to get my degree somehow, and even though I thought I deserved being denied the right to finish, I made the decision to stick it out until they insisted that I leave. You can imagine the constant strain I was under, without any let up.

Finals arrived ... it was time to graduate and get that little piece of paper which would let me proclaim to all the world that I was as good as all those others who had the lofty position of *Professional* and with a Degree to show for it, thereby proving that they *were* actually better! Headaches, heartburn and vomiting became my usual day as the end drew near. I got the news I had expected. I had flunked Dynamic Mechanics, and Alternating Circuit Theory ... both Fs! Now I definitely had nothing to crow about. I was a complete failure. The most important and valued thing to me in life was about to be denied me. The Superintendent of the Engineering College called me into his office. He also taught the Electrical Course I flunked. He inquired as to why I had done so poorly, when he thought I knew the subject enough, at least well enough to pass the final. I could graduate with one F, but I needed at least a D before I could get my certificate. With my head down in abject shame, I said I just didn't t know ... *maybe I was not smart enough.* Well, the war veteran image was still fresh with honor and respect, and I can see now that he did not have the heart to keep me from getting that final reward ... fortunately he was a real softie. He said he would make a little ten minute test, imagine my reaction, and if I passed it he would give me a D. Then I could be in the graduating line the coming weekend.

That same feeling of terror came over me and my mind was blocked. Two little questions were asked to compute a simple DC circuit that any high school physics student could easily do. Mind you, the course I was taking was Alternating Circuit Theory, which uses vector math, complex variable computations as well as other methods, but all I had to do was compute this simple DC circuit which contained rounded numbers that could be computed in the head. I know that now, but then I could only see that clock ticking away. He returned after ten minutes, smiling and cheerful, absolutely confident that I had breezed through this and had been waiting for him at least five minutes. The paper was blank. He was to say the least, shocked. *Why didn't t you work those simple formulae that you know by heart.* I could not look at him as I chokingly said with tears in my eyes, *I ... I ... ca ... ca ... can t.* With a definite tone of impatience and chagrin he said, *listen, do you know what OHMs Law is?* I replied, *Y ... Y ... Yes, Sir.* He continued, *OK, What is it?* I blurted it out, $E=IR$. He concluded, *fine ... you have a D. Now get out of here, I'm very busy.*

To this day, I have never felt that I earned that Degree, even though I have to say it did give me some status later in life with others who pride themselves for the same attainment. No one ever asked me what my average was, and of course I'd never tell. I took the first job offered to me with a big western company at $250 a month! I strove very hard as an engineer trying to invent things no one had ever thought of, and having to cow- tow to demanding bosses, as they are prone to be in big businesses. I could not seem to impress anybody. What little self esteem I had became less and less. Now it was not only headaches, heartburn and sickness; it was also bleeding stools and sometimes vomiting blood. I no longer felt young although I was but in my early thirties. Then suddenly, due to the bank taking over the company in bankruptcy, employees were being laid off. *Last in first out* was the way it went. But I knew why I was made redundant. I was no good. Not smart enough. I was a failure. How low can one get? I had married a girl who was exactly the type my parents would love. I felt I didn't deserve such a fine woman. She had a good job and helped bring home the bacon.

My Father and my Brother had both been after me for a couple of years to return home and join them running the auto agency owned by my Father, who wanted to retire; my brother, who also had a self-confidence problem, said he couldn't *do it alone,* and if we didn't t take it over our Father would sell the business. When I reported that I had lost my job, the invitation was repeated, and in complete submission I compromised my attitude that I didn't need anybody, by accepting.

My parents were literally overjoyed. There were parties with many guests, and announcements in the newspapers of my entering the business. Much fanfare! But I was very morose and ashamed that I had to depend on my parents again. I had wanted to be a huge financial success and be able to have them depend on me! I was however, with my training in engineering, able to apply much of what I learned, and even did some innovative work which was spread through the National Automotive Dealers Association or NADA, to other dealers. But somehow I still did not feel that all I had was deserved. I would not reveal this to anyone of course, and little by little, with my title, and employees always communicating to me with a Mr or a Sir, I began to enjoy a modicum of prestige, even though at heart I still felt guilty of being a fake and an undeserving leach on others.

I stayed in this secure shell under the wing of my Father and Family for about twenty years, doggedly carrying out my duties in the image of a responsible father and family man. I still had the same health problems though; migraines, stomach ulcers and nervousness, barely coping, and apprehensive of some catastrophe that was plaguing me most of the time. My exceptionally good wife of whom I never felt worthy, became permanent president of the women's division of the Church. I didn't join, mainly because I never felt I would be sincerely dedicated enough nor able to live a sufficiently pure life to call myself a Christian. Nor would I lie with the affirmations one takes when joining the Church. I could not believe what I would have to say.

My wife was the *cool* type concerning sex, and since we were both approaching forty years of age, we decided to adopt two children. One was a two days old boy; a year later the other was three days old and a girl.

AFFIRMATION ... I KNOW WHAT I AM WORTH AND I AM WORTHY

Forty Steps

Schools Out

continuing Dan's letter ...
My second joyous period in life was when my children were between one and twelve years of age. Especially the pre-school period. They truly capture the heart and that bond is forever, once

made. Even with huge differences and separations which came later, there is always that special relationship which cannot be replaced by others. *What God hath joined ...*

The business thrived. We grew accustomed to living in the *upper middle class,* as you British might say, and we also belonged to the best clubs. We put our children through the the usual juvenile organisations and my son became an Eagle Scout. We entered the teens at the same time the flower girls were operating on Haight-Ashbury; the Beatles hit America and my kids began asserting their independence.

This was the beginning of an explosion in my life. Something in me was about to burst. Questions. *Is this all there is to life. Why can't I be happy?* I had all the things that most people believe could make them happy. I saw my daughter taking off with boys in the night and heard such things as her bragging about a musician in one of the rock groups who opened his pants and played the guitar with his erect penis! Pot was being handed around and I knew that my kids were following the peer pressure to *fly baby fly.* Sex was supposed to be fun for everybody, wasn't it? I began secretly envying those very happy young people enjoying the loose life of which I had not experienced nearly enough ... or so I thought!

My daughter became pregnant. The sixties was that in-between era when it was still embarrassing to get *knocked up.* This was all unbeknownst to me, apparently because they feared some awful violence on my part. She was secreted away to New York City by my wife, for an abortion, which was illegal in those days. I was told later by the boy's father, who begged that we share the expenses of that unpleasant incident.

In my unstable state of mind, I began to think maybe that was what was the matter with the whole society. *Sexual frustration.* That was it ... certainly *part* of my problem anyway.

As the teens became bolder and bolder, Dr. Spock advised parents to let them express themselves to hopefully result in more balanced and happy beings. I smiled understandingly as my son called me a selfish bastard, and my darling daughter, adopted don't forget, began to look exceedingly luscious to me in her skimpily revealing attire. Jokes about incest were common and under the wrong circumstances I could have passed over that threshold which exists between father and lover. Thank God somehow I escaped that temptation. I really am not sure I was strong enough at that time if the opportunity had arisen. Perhaps I had a Guardian Angel who was becoming more and more real to me.

Then one day when I was particularly unhappy about the whole situation, my daughter said something to the effect that *I ought get the hell out the house anyway!* The switch turned on. That was the solution. I told her that it was the best idea I had ever heard and I would get me an apartment immediately which I did. My wife wanted to talk it over but there was nothing doing. I was beginning to feel I had to get free from it all or get smothered to death. I could afford it. I had the money. Chicks can be had with money. Young chicks. I would have orgies with very young girls ... still legal, but the younger the better. I joined a swinging sex group that met every Saturday in a motel. I was in ecstasy again. My ailments were disappearing. I was in my middle fifties and young chicks would still go out with me. Not any or all, but just enough of those luscious cute ones to keep me feeling great.

When I moved into my apartment I began dabbling into Astrology, and from that I became interested in Occultism, Sex Magic and Mind Control. I was an avid reader of anything that was far out, and especially New Age. I had joined a flying club and I took a trip to Central America. There I met a girl thirty two years younger than myself who would eventually become a big factor in making my life *brighter*. That is a story in itself. Another trip with a fellow swinger was made to Spain as part of a Real Estate Promotion, and on impulse I bought an apartment there before returning home.

Still playing with young girls, I took a lovely 18 year old on a two week steamship trip to France. We were to buy a Camper in Paris and she was going to decorate the apartment and we would tour Europe from there. A beautiful plan which was never to be.

The second day out on this staid old British ship, she disappeared. That girl, being a model on occasions, was the prettiest and sexiest thing on the ship. We travelled first class which meant most of our fellow travellers were old people.

There were plenty of young people down below decks in the third class section. That was where the life was! I could just see what was happening. The young guys couldn't believe she was with me and wondered if maybe she was my daughter. There are more lurid details, but the meat of it all was: She stayed hidden with the third classers until the day before we were due to land in France, apparently, because all had their fun with her and none planned to take care of her after landing. She came back and turned all her charm on me ... she could certainly do that ... and wanted me to forgive her so we could continue the trip as planned. I had time to ponder the statistics of an eighteen year old ravishing blond girl with a fifty six year old tired out OLD man! An old duffa, as you Brits might colloquially put it.

I was thankful and satisfied that I had even gotten that last shot, but I still left her crying on the dock in Cherbourg and told her some very nasty things about her treatment of me. I went onwards to Spain as planned, with a chap I had met on the boat, and we became close friends up to his death some years later. The girl wrote me a letter when she got back. She had gotten help from her parents through the U.S. Consulate and apologized profusely ... we had both learned our lessons!

AFFIRMATION ... I LIVE WITH INTEGRITY

Graduation Day

continuing Dan's letter ...

I had moved more or less permanently to Spain by now and imported as companions the few remaining bed mates I had contact with in the U.S. One by one, each of these became disagreements and disappointments, leaving me alone once again. I was going downhill rapidly in mind and body. I had met a German in Spain who liked to travel. I came down with a terrible neuritis in my arm one December ... Spain *can* become very cold. I was frantic to get warm. The girl I had met in Costa Rica wrote me a letter and said she would come to my side if I would send her a ticket. I wrote that my German friend and I were going down to Morocco to get warm and when I got back I would send for her. My friend and I stayed longer than expected. When we got back to Spain, three letters were waiting for me from Costa Rica ... *Why had I deceived her?* Immediately, I sent the 'plane ticket, and this was the beginning of the most important phase of my life.

I had also gotten involved in a spiritual cult in France, which eventually led me to England. I was at the nadir of interest in this life. All seemed pointless. She arrived like a warm Spring breeze. Her youth and vivaciousness absolutely lifted me up into feeling alive again! I have said it and will say it many times again ... *she radiated so much unconditional love, like I had never experienced before, that she filled my empty heart to overflow, so that I, for the first time in my lengthening life, actually experienced loving someone else; namely her.* I was suspicious at first, thinking she would surely dump me like the rest, but over these twenty some years her enthusiastic *I love yous* practically every day has made a believer out of me. I have never met anyone like her. She is precious to me ... perhaps an angel from heaven.

We travelled to Sri Lanka on a six month trip in the camper, with my German friend, living in the wilds of Turkey, Afghanistan and India; bathing in rivers and living as free as the wind. We visited several Ashrams, as I had great interest in Kirpal Singh who was supposedly a *Master of Eckankar,* Sai Baba who was supposedly the *Christ for India,* and Ramana Maharshi, *the last of the Great Living Saints.*

When we returned I realized I was really in love ... like you read about in story books. I'd been hit by a lingering thunderbolt! We are soul mates, like we've known each other in previous lives ... like I am trying to pay a karmic debt to her and my age means nothing.

She accompanied me to France and I began my activities in the cult mentioned previously. This was an important section of my life, since part of their activity involved mental processes which cause one to review one's life, and or lives, as related to the unwanted feelings most of us have. To be brief, although it took seven years of my life, I did erase, with reviewing and understanding, most of the powerful feelings and considerations that I had placed on myself, and I am not in the least sorry about my involvement with that cult, even though I am more than suspicious about its financial aspirations and most of its higher level stuff.

However, that was accomplished in the first year or two, and during the remaining four or five years of my membership, I became disillusioned with the dedication demanded by the organization, and sadly suspicious about the founder. I felt trapped, and for a long time did not know how to resign gracefully. I was like the man who had mixed feelings about his mother-in-law going over the cliff *in his Cadillac.*

Since that time, my life has grown into a beautiful experience. An analogy could be a white water rafting ride ... being tossed, spilled, nearly drowned, and then drifting onto the big wide, calm and beautiful lake. As I review my life now, I realise that I have let go of all irrelevancies in favour of real personal development. Spiritual development. Improving the Being.

Is it for everyone?

I am not qualified to answer that. I still occasionally get thoughts about how fortunate and lucky I have been, always silently expressing my thanks maybe several times a day, and I can still get piqued about how I seemed to have had so little to do with it. The harder I tried to be a strong and self sufficient person, the worse my life turned out. I have spent the last ten to fifteen years doing much meditation, talking to God, or, communing with That I Am, or, whatever it is for each individual. It seems that there are forces, entities or whatever you wish to call them, guiding me, and if I just relax and affirm in my meditations that I want to be a tool for Good or Divine Purpose things just happen to me like magic. As I said to you over the phone Phil ... some of these *things* seem downright spooky!

It is natural that I, having passed my eightieth birthday, should be looking more towards the time of passing over than someone of your age Phil. There is nothing wrong with that as long as I don't get morbid about it. We don t want an infant to be pondering these things. As Ecclesiastes the preacher, said ... *there is a time and place for each thing* ... or words to that effect. There is a slow metamorphosis in living and growing. Wouldn't it be fascinating to see a time lapse photographic playback of an entire life!

Of course I have left out many stories within my story. Anyone's life could fill volumes. I don't feel I've done too good a job with this writing thing, but in keeping with the theme of your book I can say the brightness in my life seemed to be handed to me, and was not due to anything I did, unless one could say I chose finally, to simply let go and *let God.* I am also a millionaire if the term equates with being rich. Rich in spiritual feeling and acceptance however, and not in the financial sense.

It is something which makes me feel very humble and extremely grateful to Whomever or Whatever is running this show.

173

As I read your first draft, and the other stories in it, I see a common thread running throughout, which we would probably see in anyone's story. It is difficult to define, but perhaps something along the line that *all of us have this searching for something that secretly hides within us. Is it knowledge, understanding, reliable data, an attitude, state of mind, feeling, emotion, or several or all of these?*

Here I am once again humbly admitting my ignorance. How can we communicate fully, an experience or a goal to another? The classic example of our inability to put in words what we experience is when we try relating to an innocent virgin what an orgasm feels like. No *second hand knowledge* can equal the *first hand experience* of knowing. I am really grateful and honored that you asked me to contribute to your book. How often does a person get the chance to relate their life story to someone that is interested enough to request it. Most of us seem to feel that no one cares or wants to listen. Your book could carry an open invitation to all readers ... to submit *their* stories for future inspirational books. Gads! What a source of material for an author of novels! You would never run out of themes Phil. And just submitting one's story in wide open un-ashamed honesty could be very therapeutic to more than a few. I know because that is what I have just done and can vouch for the validity of the exercise.

I surely had not planned to write all this as you can see from my first paragraph. But now it's done it's done. Edit it, paraphrase it ... do whatever you wish with it!

I think you are writing in a really helpful track Phil, which will benefit many people who know it, and others who perhaps don't yet know it.

Wishing you love and forgiveness,
Dan

AFFIRMATION ... I LOVE AND FORGIVE

Forty Two Steps

Within You Without You

We were talking - about the space between us all
And the people - who hide themselves behind a wall of illusion
Never glimpse the truth - then it's far too late - when they pass away.
We were talking - about the love we all could share - when we find it
To try our best to hold it there - with our love
With our love - we could save the world - if they only knew.
Try to realise it's all within yourself no-one else can make you change
And to see you're really only very small,
and life flows on within you and without you.
We were talking - about the love that's gone so cold and the people,
Who gain the world and lose their soul - they don't know -
they can't see - are you one of them?
When you've seen beyond yourself - then you may find peace of mind is
waiting there -
And the time will come when you see we're all one and life flows on
within you and without you.

This song, which was on The Beatles *Sgt. Pepper's Lonely Hearts Club Band* album originally released in 1967, is the most complete depiction of true personal development that I have ever come across. Even more remarkable is the fact that these vivid lyrics form a song by fitting beautifully into the Indian style music which supports them.

The words that George Harrison utilised were undoubtedly inspired by his involvement at the time with eastern philosophy, Transcendental Meditation, and perhaps his then teacher or guru, The Maharishi Mahesh Yogi.

Whether the influence be eastern or western is irrelevant for our purpose of inculcating ourselves with just enough data to allow our own personal stories to shine through ... and when they shine, they shine bright, and all around is illuminated. Brightening your own life is a service to others also. All improvement has a ripple, or knock on effect.

It is worth noting that more time was spent by the PeRFECT WORDS and MUSIC office in securing permission to reprint these lyrics than with any other single part of the research for this book. The Northern Songs catalogue to which this song belongs, is currently owned by Michael Jackson; *as I edit the text I noticed that this catalogue has been sold once again;* the publishing is administered by EMI, and the print sales by a company called Music Sales. *Where does George Harrison fit into this picture?* I hear you think.

When permission finally arrived, the fee was so high that we had to think twice about the necessity to reproduce them in their entirety. We decided that it was important enough, but still telephoned the person responsible for dealing in such matters and secured a 75% reduction in fees. It's a tough old world in business, and I have been told that only the tigers survive!

The lyrics are perfect for the culmination of this level we call The Graduate. I believe they also summarise the final part of Dan's letter which precedes them. No certificate or diploma will ever be awarded to you for inner achievement. No teacher can ever give you a tick or a star for a successful TTM, and of course we must acknowledge that not all steps along the personal development trail are clearcut or well defined.

Your success depends on *you* and *you alone.* You cannot ever blame external circumstances for unhappiness once you are cognisant of the ageless wisdom which states quite clearly that true happiness is an *inner* feeling of satisfaction. You can affirm and inculcate into your very beingness, *all that is good,* but if you are not living your story, the results will at best be second rate.

That is why this, my fourth personal development book, is

about the storyteller which lives in us all. *You ARE the stories you tell,* and we are all capable of living great stories. Don't ever measure your story by external personality type yardsticks. They do not work on real happiness. Inside we are all Buddha and Christ and God and Love ... we need no external affirmation of these simple facts ... just inner knowing and a little practice with *Time To Myself.* All will be revealed if you are not too busy! A little time spent peeling back a layer which has veiled the treat behind your personality is surely worth giving to yourself.

Your story is your happiness. Whatever it is ... it is yours. It is unique and it is your only reason for being. Live it, enjoy it, for *you are your story and that story is you!*

AFFIRMATION ... MY HAPPINESS WITHIN ENSURES MY HAPPINESS WITHOUT

Reflection

A glimpse of someone else's story can stimulate each of us to revue our own. As Dan intonated, a few stories together could make an inspirational book. Maybe you would like to send me yours .. whether it be written in advance or in retrospect, it may contain that vital stimulation others have been waiting for to launch novels of their own.

Following your nose can be as useful as it was for The Wayward Sheep ... NOT ... or it can involve an evocation of personal intuition, which itself has to be nurtured. Naturally I do not advocate the former and I do encourage the latter. Whatever you follow, you should follow it in your story ... those wishing to be stimulated by the stories of others', may like to read Voltaire's story of Candide ... inspiration is truly a wonderful gift and it is there for us all to cherish.

AFFIRMATIONS

I QUESTION MYSELF ... I WRITE MY OWN STORY BEFORE IT HAPPENS ... I AM CONFIDENT ... I KNOW WHAT I AM WORTH AND I AM WORTHY ... I LIVE WITH INTEGRITY ... I LOVE AND FORGIVE ... MY HAPPINESS WITHIN ENSURES MY HAPPINESS WITHOUT

Live totally, and live intensely, so that each moment becomes golden and your whole life becomes a series of golden moments. Such a person never dies because he has the Midas touch: Whatever he touches becomes golden ...

Osho

The Storyteller

Forty Three Steps

Killer Queen

Six thousand seven hundred years ago, a griffin was born. Now what I am about to tell you of this griffin cannot be proved true or false, and that is the way both the griffin and myself wish it to be. As my words cannot be corroborated in any way, if I tell you that this griffin still lives and intends to remain in physical incarnation until he reaches seven thousand years of age, you must rely on my integrity, as I have relied upon the integrity of what you may consider to be a mythical creature.

I know you are thinking that I am perhaps stretching the reader's imagination by describing a creature of such history, but that is only the beginning. If you struggle to accept my words at this early stage I am uncertain if the unfoldment of this story will either help you concede to it, or turn you from my writing altogether ... *que sera sera, whatever will be will be* ... those griffins were a philosophical lot way back when, and whether they remained that way, only the unfoldment of this story will tell.

Griffins had no use for names, and our friend will therefore be known only by his initial of G. If you noticed the possessive pronoun already utilised, you will now think yourself cognisant of our hero's gender. However, he was a girl and she was a boy ... griffins reproduced themselves without any of that messy business which involves pairs in the human kingdom. In that Queendom of

179

the Killers, only the basilisks bred as entertainment for the royalty. The basilisks were fabulous reptiles no longer than half a metre. They would readily kill men just by looking at them, but never women. Just why this was so is not for the forty third step. Suffice to say that their habits were precisely the reason why the Queens allowed them to exist.

The point is that G was part of a breed despised for their curiosity, and worshipped for their knowledge. They were a living paradox who followed tradition just enough to stimulate further inquisitiveness. Their keepers were a line of lords who cloned one another. They ate constantly and although only one lord ever lived at one moment in time, they were all called Lord Gula; their over consumption of comestibles was irritating to others, and indeed caused early death in each of them.

The adjectivity of the Queendom so far, may lead you to believe that it was a gloomy place, but that would be subjective observation and utterly useless for accurate understanding. It was, in actual fact, a happy place. Birth and death were of no consequence. The pursuit of pleasure was sufficient reason for the Queens *to be,* the consumption of food was the purpose of the Lords Gula and the death of men satisfied the basilisks. This leaves G and his breed without enough description ... so ... they lived according to a verbal recounting of their purpose, which was secret. Esoteric in the main and only exoteric secondarily; this is all I can tell you before we proceed with what happened to G.

The griffins were relative newcomers to the Queendom, arriving from Europe after the Gibraltar Strait had been breached by the Atlantic Ocean to form that middle sea known as the Mediterranean. It was rumoured that they fled from Atlantis just before it had been submerged, but no one could ever prove it. They brought with them European ways which frequently caused dismay amongst other breeds, most of which I have not described as I do not have adequate information about them.

You must know a little about Gs appearance and the following will suffices: all griffins have the body and legs of a lion, the head and wings of an eagle, and most importantly, listening ears. They have strength and agility, but their chief attribute is watchfulness. They are both clairvoyant and clairaudient, and if you are used to the analogy often drawn between the age of a dog and that of a human, and it is that each human year signifies seven of a dog, then that would not prove useful in objectifying a griffin's years ... more like each griffin year being equivalent to one human sniff during a tiresome bout of influenza. That just about describes them, for when they pass out of this physical life after seven thousand years of breathing, they are unaware of any change in their circumstances.

So, one day G was told *the griffin way* and it is this ... for the first two thousand one hundred year part of a griffin's life, it is considered essential to design the life in a visionary way from a blueprint which griffins innately comprehend, just as it is expected to be, although from a youthful perspective. The next two thousand one hundred years are spent working the blueprint and honing the rough edges from each individual plan. For the following two thousand one hundred years a griffin will indeed discover himself and his God, before concluding his breathing life by teaching all he knows for the last two thousand one hundred years.

Close observers of fact will by now have deduced that this arithmetic cannot be correct; either I am wrong or you are, and fortunately it is you. You see, a griffin teaches all he knows firstly whilst breathing, and secondly when discarnate, when he forms the great astral classrooms of our dream world, in a faculty of knowledge. Very useful creatures these griffins, and as they understand that teaching all you know also helps self- inculcation of information, they go about their occupations quite unlike an employee of a state run business and more like a self employed person expanding his precious company.

It rarely happens, but when *the griffin way* is not completely understood, it does cause a partial wastage of opportunity. Their culture was oral and we must be thankful that ours utilises the written word, which *can* be physically revisited for clarification. The griffin has no such opportunity as the culture is explained once and once only. Because of this adherence to tradition, G remained unaware of the innate ability to contact his blueprint and was consequently unaware of his story. He was a griffin of unparalleled energy however, and even though ignorant of this fundamental issue, he went about his business with gusto and impressed Lord Gula so much that he was allowed what a griffin, like the aborigine, calls walkabout, much earlier than otherwise would have been the case.

So it was that G transcended the etheric womb of that Queendom of the Killers; clever, energetic, hopeful and ever eager to increase his knowledge using that inherent tool of good fortune known as curiosity. After a banquet where the basilisks ate some men and some men ate some animals and the Lord Gula ate whatever was placed in front of him, G, using his wings for the very first time, flew out from the protective forcefield which had surrounded him since birth and hit the great sky roads with wide open eyes.

AFFIRMATION ... MY ATTENTION IS POWERFUL

Forty Four Steps
                    Court Of The Crimson King

Now it is not to be supposed that G flew straight from that queendom to the kingdom mentioned in this title, for that would be misleading. It would be correct however, to indicate that G found little of interest to a griffin, until he arrived at that Court Of The Crimson King. He had few experiences worthy of mention and no friends whatsoever to show for his travels up until that point. Perhaps it was because the kingdom reminded him of years gone by, or maybe less mysteriously that it was located where Egypt now finds itself, and that being close to Europe from whence the griffin breed first came. The relevance is that a feeling sprang up from within him, and nothing the Lord Gula had told him during the oral recital of *the griffin way* could explain it.

He began asking questions as only a griffin can, and soon brought out the worst in those who listened to him, for it was not *the way* in that kingdom to answer the questions of any foreigner, let alone one who flew like an eagle and roared like a lion. It was not long before he was sentenced to death for *being aggravating,* as it stated on the charge sheet.

Now as you can imagine, G had no fear of death as it is not part of the mythology for that breed to which he belongs. Death to him would be similar to the sudden and violent death of a human. In other words, he would not know about it. The analogy weakens however, as time from the point of decease lengthens. If a human was driving to an important meeting in connection with his business, and he had the misfortune to fall fatal victim to a violent road offence involving sudden death for him, he would indeed carry on travelling to his meeting, taking his seat and making his contribution. It would only be after much frustration at not being heard or acknowledged in any way, that the reality of his death would begin to dawn. Only those clairvoyant or clairaudient would be aware of any presence.

G on the other hand, would firstly know of his imminent passing into existence without breath, and secondly is capable of carrying on his business as normal, even if that means frightening a few in other breeds by being *spooky*. He could not foresee his own death being imminent, and therefore asked to be presented to The Crimson King.

Of course the goalers laughed and scoffed at his innocence, but they were scheduled to eat crow it seems, because very soon after

G asked this supposed naive question, the king coincidentally decided on a spontaneous inspection of the royal dungeons, where much to his half surprise, he found G sitting on his hind legs, wings neatly folded, sporting a smile The Buddha would have found attractive if he had lived two thousand five hundred years prior and in that area.

We know each other don't we? stated G half questioningly.

Silence, shouted the guard with a crack of his whip.

Yes, answered the king.

Why are you crimson? asked G without fear.

Because, answered the king, *I survived Atlantis. Some were spared the catastrophe and found their way here to seed a new race. I was sentenced to death, and die I very nearly did, for indeed I sank with the continent. I was a black magician and revelled in my own sorcery. Now sadly my powers have lessened in exact ratio to the amount I used them for work in evil. I am young sir, crimson because I surfaced too quickly from three miles beneath the ocean. These slits you may have noticed in my neck, are gills created with my last burst of power to outwit the sentence imposed on me.*

And are you happy that this last burst of power has lengthened your breathing life? came the swift follow up question from G.

Ha, replied the king, *happy? I am utterly miserable. In Atlantis I was stretched to the limits of my intelligence. Here I am a shadow of that giant. It is only because these stupid wretches are without brains that I am able to rule.*

So what then is the reason behind the symptoms that you describe for your unhappiness? asked G.

I shouldn't be here! replied the king sporting an ironic smile, *I was scheduled to die and dead I should be. That was the plan and I sought to defy it which I did!*

G pondered the kings words whilst reminding him that imprisonment and execution were not part of his plans. The king understood and executed the guard instead, for his impertinence. G remembered from where he knew The Crimson King and it was indeed Atlantis, although he could not prove it. It was during the pre breathing etheric existence that he remembered this character. G was still working legitimately in the astral realms and the king, who was not a king then, was using the astral world of desire to get what he wanted from the lesser lives. G recalled challenging him, but that was all ... the memory was hazy and irrelevant.

G was still pondering the kings words ... *I shouldn't be here* ... when all of a sudden the earth moved and he was transported without the aid of his wings, through the tornados and whirlwinds of almighty space, before landing elsewhere some two thousand odd years later.

AFFIRMATION ... I AM WHERE I SHOULD BE

Forty Five Steps

Einstein A Gogo

G was getting older, and he hinted to his higher self that this ageing was due to an occurrence beyond his control; it was agreed and G realised that this was normal. His wings ached a little more than normal, and he knew better than to make them perform tricks of youth. This, his will power *would* allow, but he knew that the body would crumple and serve no useful function in so doing.

It was around seventeen hundred years ago. The winds settled and the dust was still. He let out an almighty roar in Alexandria and someone appeared to discover what the fuss was about. It was

Ptolemy, or so he said, and without so much as a how are you, he launched straight into the most far reaching question G had ever been asked ... *what is your purpose, why the noise, and are the two connected?*

G was pleasantly taken aback, for, although he was not used to such forwardness, it certainly caused him no offence. G tuned to the carrier wave of communication rather than the actual words. This method served him nicely and his meeting with Ptolemy was to prove no exception. Ptolemy used Gs pondering of his earlier question to comment on the appearance of what stood before him ... *you are indeed unsightly; in fact you remind me of an unattractive dog; no offence intended you understand, but I have to comment on the fact that you are not normal.*

How do you know I am unattractive, replied G with a smile that defied any negative conclusion, *and to what scale of reference are you alluding when you make such observations?*

Ptolemy was thrilled. A mind of similar if not greater magnitude to his own. *I don't need any scale to know you are ugly,* Ptolemy continued, *you are an ugly little runt of a something, but I will not hold that against you ... even though I may have to look elsewhere occasionally when talking with you.* Ptolemy calmed himself before speaking further to his new acquaintance ... *My eyes are weak ... they spend so much time gazing at heavenly bodies that I am afraid they are now no earthly good. I am sir, an astronomer! What are you, and as I said in my introduction, what is your purpose and why so much noise?*

G thought for a moment, which irritated Ptolemy who was used to great respect and quick communications from the sycophantic people who surrounded him ... *I am a griffin* ... was the simplistic reply ... *my purpose seems to be curiosity and the noise was due to the dust for which I cannot take responsibility, even though it was me who roared with irritation. Any connection between emanations of noise from me and my purpose as you put it, is for you to deduce, as you acquaint yourself with me, if that is YOUR purpose!*

The two bandied words for quite sometime, and despite their obvious intelligence, there was a voracious game of one up manship occurring just beneath the apparent placidity of clever words and exchanged concepts. The question as to Gs purpose in life aggravated him so much that he steered all conversation clear of the subject lest he be found out.

What have you discovered up there in our sky, asked G of Ptolemy, *and what significance does it have?*

Ptolemy replied quickly with an answer he always had at the ready for that question ... *Scientists, philosophers and astronomers have opened the minds of everyone to space travel. Old Aristotle, who was around four hundred years ago, said that our earth is the centre of this universe, and that it is a sphere because its shadow is curved as it falls across the moon during an eclipse. I have made great advances on Aristotle's work and have now recorded the position of more than one thousand stars and divided them into constellations.*

G smiled, but knew there was more to Ptolemy than met his eye. To Gs naive and simplistic way of thinking, space travel already existed, witnessed by anyone watching him flying ... *what is your purpose for such great work my friend?* he asked, kicking himself at mentioning that word purpose again.

Purpose, purpose, why space travel of course, replied Ptolemy, *society is as great as it has creative people within it. Tomorrow is dreamed by artists, scientists and indeed any people showing signs of great purpose. I never regret yesterday, I celebrate life today whilst helping create our tomorrows!*

The griffin knew he had just heard a great reply which helped him both to understand why so many people around Ptolemy were sycophants, and also why his definition of space travel was inferior to the one which must have been held by this great philosopher. *Well, if you forgive me sir, can I ask why you are involved in an occupation which cannot possibly see its conclusion before your short human incarnation is ended?*

Because that is my purpose, replied Ptolemy with a slightly pretentious laugh, *which reminds me of my earlier question to you ...*

G steadied himself by rudely speaking over his friends words ... *do you believe in my clairvoyance?* G noted an affirmative nod of his friends head; *then I must say you will be successful ...*

Ptolemy remonstrated, no no no no no .... *shut up you ugly little runt! What is the point of knowing the conclusion? My work will have no purpose to it from a human standpoint if you reveal too many details of what I already intuitively know to be a successful conclusion. I predict that we shall land on that moon you see above us in the year 1640. This year coincides with the first showing of a new energy which will make itself available to earth. By the year two thousand we shall all see into each other's minds and physical talk will cease as a necessity. This will be the Aquarian Age, the successor of this Piscean Age. All will be love and love will be all! I am tempted to ask just how right I am, but I will not, so please say no more about this and come take some herb drink with me; it should settle your roar and help you see me as a good person.*

As Ptolemy took his first drink, he dropped down dead. It was many hours before their conversation ended however, and G consoled Ptolemy as the cognition of death hit him with a jolt. G suspected that local justice may not look upon him kindly and he found a cave by the sea which could not be reached by anyone without wings, closed his eyes and meditated. He saw the seventeenth century and woke up to its actuality. His wings needed a good stretch and he flew to England via Italy.

It was the year 1642 when he witnessed the death of Galileo. They spent a year together during which he allowed G to use his telescope and explained the moons of Jupiter. As those around cried and mourned and complained and wondered at the death of such a great man, G would hear nothing of it as he began to sense some link between episodes in his life. He felt that a great birth was occurring as the soul of Galileo passed through the heavens and into devachan, where blissful rest would be available to him for fifteen hundred earth years if he wished.

G continued his journey to England, where he helped a young lady bring forth a baby into this world whom she named Isaac. The Newtons were happy and unaware of any involvement in their affairs by a griffin. Isaac grew accustomed to an awareness of G, and G passed on as much intuitive data to Isaac as the lad could take. Newton felt inspired and conceded that inspiration was a tiring inflow of energy. G was elated to be performing a good purpose and conceded that such purpose was essential for happiness to be forthcoming.

Gravity was discovered by Newton, but G did not celebrate as he could not understand any ignorance of such law. When his wings ached and he ceased flapping them he descended; when he was fit and he flapped them he ascended. That was *the griffin law of gravity* which he slowly understood to have been the inspiration for Newton to have verbalised *the human law of gravity* and lay the foundations of modern astronomy.

G thought of Ptolemy and wondered if he watched from his rest. 1640 had passed without man landing on the moon; Galileo was dead and now Newton was dying. G let out a sigh which was a roar and thought of Albert Einstein. Gs last great meditation of the seventeen hundreds brought a clear foresight ... *space and time co-exist as spacetime which can be imagined as a rubber sheet that stretches as objects are placed on it, giving a hint that one day time travel might become possible!*

What would the Crimson King have made of that?

AFFIRMATION ... I HELP OTHERS WITH THEIR STORIES

Forty Six Steps
                    The Whole Of The Moon

Two hundred years of nothing, G wrote in his diary. He contemplated his existence in disgust and vowed it to be better. After noting the improvements that had been made in glass, thought, metals and construction, he again reflected on those human incarnations now so far away in the past, and wondered what *they* would make with these new materials *and* with the help of all this new technology which seemed to be everywhere. As G thought of these things, Edwin Hubble began building the Hubble Telescope in his mind. *There are galaxies beyond the milky way,* said Hubble to G, *and they are moving away from us as the universe expands.* It was 1923 and Einstein had been alive for many years. His theory of relativity, which people became aware of in 1915, seemed remarkably similar to Gs earlier meditations.

What did all this mean, G pondered.

As the griffin began a more etheric existence during the 1960s, he was glad to see Doctor Who travelling through time and space in his Tardis. H G Wells would have been thankful, and perhaps the Russians were appreciative of *all* earlier efforts, as the Soviet cosmonaut Yuri Gagarin became the first man in non television space, and thus demonstrated for the first time the theories of all those earlier philosophers.

Ptolemy rolled over in his devachan and readied himself for

another stint on earth. On that day in 1969, when Neil Armstrong and Buzz Aldrin landed on our moon, Ptolemy was again born. G noted the rapidly increasing speed of noteworthy events which had begun to occur. Through remaining with the spirit of Edwin Hubble, he was instrumental in the launching of the Hubble Telescope into space.

G knew what would happen and Hubble proved him right. That telescope produced findings which defied many human conceptions about the universe, and showed that a mysterious force was indeed at work. *What is this mysterious force,* thought G.

After many transient relationships and some light friendships, G began yearning for a soul mate. Spiritual friendship was much talked about but little practiced, and this turn of the century time period which heralded the Aquarian Age, and caused many to think of love without necessarily demonstrating it, was a strange old time. It was even stranger for G as he gradually began the normal griffin process of further dematerialisation. His existence was now totally etheric, and he was sensed by fewer and fewer people as each day passed, although it must be said that these numbers began increasing after their initial decline.

1996 dawned, and as preparations were discussed about celebrations for the turning of the millennium, G watched an aged friend called Mn, build an energy body from etheric material. This old friend was indeed an ancient soul and went about his business methodically and meticulously. He knew that his imminent incarnation would only be as useful as he had an efficient etheric body, so in this task he devoted much time. He was never too busy to talk to an old friend however, and as they sat on a star, the following conversation occurred ...

You are indeed an old friend, he said to G with warmth, *we go all the way back to Atlantean times, and I even have recollection of you before, during that long forgotten life period of Lemuria.*

During Adamic and Hyperborean times, I guess we must have been getting prepared for life on this planet at the same time, and now here we sit on a star, chewing the fat, shooting the breeze and mulling the past.

G was pleased to be with his old friend but had a burning question, *what happened to the Master Jesus?*

I can see that you have been alive during the last two thousand years, through that one question, replied Mn, and what does it matter? The Master Jesus was ahead of his contemporaries in evolutionary terms. He had many great lives, the last of which he sacrificed the first thirty or so years, so that the one we followed during Atlantean times called The Christ, could influence life through the body of Jesus, as Christ's advancement prohibited life through birth. Jesus lives in the same body now as he did then, in Syria I think, and he is an initiate of the fifth degree. The Christ is now too strong an energy to inhabit a human body of any strength, even if that was karmically permitted. He is therefore scheduled to appear as an influence on many groups. His energy will thus be diluted, making it much more suitable for human utilisation. The life for which I now prepare, will be as a disciple of Christ, even though I will rarely even utter his name, let alone voice my purpose in such terms

Well this really is interesting, said G, willing Mn to continue, *and what will his message be this time?*

Same old thing, replied Mn, *Love.*

G once again recalled the great Ptolemy's words ... *This will be the Aquarian Age, the successor of this Piscean Age. All will be love and love will be all!* He could not help marvel at the integration of so many disparate people from a diversity of ages, being aware of such similar messages. Even though he was clairvoyant, he was only able to see wavelengths to which he was in tune. This still therefore allowed for admiration in others when they could see future events of such beauty. G ventured another question ... *will we be privileged to see this being called The Christ?*

If you want, replied Mn simply.

AFFIRMATION ... I AM AN IMPORTANT PART OF THE UNIVERSE

Forty Seven Steps
                    Stairway To Heaven

G was pleased at his good fortune in being friends with such an intuitive and knowing being as Mn. Even though they went back a long way to the old days, G noted that there was no sentimentality attached to the words of Mn and this observation formed the substance of Gs next question ... *do you believe in the past?*

Mn hugged his friend, *you are the past, present and future G; I see you note that I speak with little or no affection for the past, but this is out of respect and not malice. My only sentimentality is for the future my old friend, and I contribute to the successful working out of The Plan ... yes, that is the result I wish to see ... success!*

These were strange words for the griffin to hear, yet, they stimulated him in an uncanny manner to which he was singularly unacquainted. *I hear the words Mn, but I do not understand; what is this plan you speak of?*

With minds tuned to one another, G and his friend Mn, jumped down from the star on which they had sat, and thought their way to London. Hovering around the City, where all that important business was begun, worked out and concluded, Mn criticised the workings of humanity for a while before making some observations ... *Look and learn G, look at humanity and deduce ...*

despite the high cost of living, it remains popular; they think they are mistaken but they are mistaken; they are not young enough to know everything ... their minds are made up so do not confuse them with facts ... no matter where they go, there they are ... they guarantee psychotherapy, or your mania back ... they have to exercise free will as they have no choice ... a clear conscience is merely the result of bad memory ... the trouble with the alcoholics is they do not remain anonymous ... today is the tomorrow they were worried about yesterday ... if they have to choose between two evils, they inevitably choose the one they haven't tried before ... if they are not confused, they are not well informed ... even moderation down there is practiced to excess ... those who laugh last just do not understand the joke ... their finest speeches have good beginnings and good endings very close together ... it would be far better to light a small candle than for them to curse the darkness ... success is getting what they want, but they must understand that happiness is wanting what they get ... work is the curse of the drinking class ... a human diplomat is a man who thinks twice before he says nothing ... the only humans never disappointed are those who expect nothing ... if only they were half as sure of anything as some people are of everything ... they don't die down there, they just under-achieve; you see G, everything has a beginning, a middle and an end; a start, a change and a stop; an inspiration, a transformation and a conclusion; all these people you see scurrying around being busy, are working through their own plans, yet few of them have spent the time to contact and study just what those plans may be. The people they work for may have spent a little more time pondering their purposes, but often not. They all frequently complain about the governments they democratically elected, and some even blame these administrations for the unworkability of their own personal plans. Gads, it goes on and on G.

The microcosms of the macrocosm!

G frowned a note of misunderstanding which was addressed by

194

Mn as follows ...

There is much lacking in the griffin way my friend; you pass on orally so little of what is, that I am surprised your breed have survived as long as they have with what was.

There is in this great universe of ours, a grand edict known as The Law of Correspondence, which states simply ... AS ABOVE SO BELOW; AS BELOW SO ABOVE. *These humans whom we watch for instance, they are in actual fact exact replicas of greater creations. As a human conceives of a metaphor, ignorance remains an order of the day concerning the greater cosmic metaphor coined by a greater being in the sky, of which each member of humanity is a part. Even the ovum as it travels down the fallopian tube of a female, rotates as does a planet. The human being rules over the universe which is the body, as does the sun with its solar system and the planetary logos over its physical manifestation which in this case is the planet earth.*

Some people believe the great earth spirit to be God; others see God as the spirit manifesting our sun as the light which shines on all alike. But who is God to our sun, and who is God to that God? If you think and meditate along these lines you will come across a ring pass not of thought. But, if you persist with this line of thinking, you will create a critical mass which will demand an inspiration, impossible to think with concrete brains, as we may describe them with respect.

As we all evolve spiritually, we allow ourselves more and more insight into The Great Law of Correspondence, which takes us higher and higher in our contemplative activity until we are all eventually one; for it is as one that we are all God, and it is as individuals that we must all become cognisant of THE ONE LIFE.

So you see G, all of these people running here, there and everywhere, doing this, that and the other, worshipping him, her and that, wondering who, where and how, only need stop for a while to discover their real purpose for life on this planet called earth, and lives will indeed be transformed ... not in the sensational ways which would be of interest to their tabloid newspapers you know ... I talk here of inner peace and tranquillity. If a human is willing to spend time alone, looking inward to the inner world of spirit, they will discover that God lives in each and everyone of us ... there is a Christ within each, and a Buddha in all. But alas G, they are mostly too busy to find the one thing which they all seek.

G was transfixed, but knew that Mn was touching on subject matter which was delicate to say the least, as he knew that a great non-confront existed within him connected to this matter of raison d'être, or, reason for being. He had a question worthy of interrupting the flow of Mns words and it was this ... *is there anything greater than God, Mn?*

Mn cleared his throat and plucked some energy from the ether, which he hinted would be useful for his next Heart Centre ... *greater than God you ask ... greater, greater? Perhaps not greater G, and this is indeed a delicate matter of which we speak. Such words would be deeply offensive to many we watch working below us in the City down there. Then again, perhaps yes, there is one thing greater than God, and it is The Plan which emanated from the mind of God. Philosophers may disagree, but my thought patterns are here connected with the subject of evolution.*

If the purpose of God is to splinter into a myriad of sparks, whilst remaining integral you understand, for the purpose of gaining in-form-ation with which to enjoy the bliss of nothingness even more after a reintegration of all those beautiful sparks, then the resultant whole would indeed be greater than the initial emanation. The Plan is therefore potentially greater than God, and that is your answer my friend!

G was stunned by the wisdom and became uncharacteristically

humble, whilst maintaining an amount of decorum. *Is there anything greater than the Plan then?* G continued with his incessant curiosity.

Now that you mention it G, and following my previous line of reasoning, the answer must once again be YES! Mn thought a little longer than usual before continuing. *Just as God emanates The Plan from his mind as a point of light, he also emanates a point of love from his heart. From these two actualities all humanity must work towards a final reunion with The All which is God. The Great Law of Correspondence means that as God has a story, so must each individual member of humanity have a story, and it is these stories which are greater than God and The Plan alike. For, these stories, all zilliontrillion and gobledeegookquadrillion of them, are the greatest of all ever, for they will form The Greatest Story Ever Told, and it is to this story that we all aspire.*

With these words, and his Heart Centre firmly built into a most loving bundle, Mn was born once again. Sudden as his departure was, G understood, for when incarnation calls, few are able to delay the process without very good reason. G thought love and Mn knew it. The time had arrived for our griffin friend to confront the unconfrontable, and for this purpose, G knew it was time to be alone for what happened next.

AFFIRMATION ... I MAKE MY OWN HEAVEN

Forty Eight Steps

Roll With It

G roamed the heavens which were now so readily accessible for him and revelled somewhat in the expansion of his own consciousness. He felt however, that this expansion was due to an inflow from Mn rather than an outflow from G. Both flows were good, he understood, but a balance was imperative for long term gain.

Just what he hoped to gain was the subject of his next meditation, during which he inadvertently stumbled on the Christ within, just after he had encountered the Buddha within. Now these were not startling revelations like one may have been programmed to expect; they were more a further and deeper understanding of *The Grand Scheme Of Things*. After he had become aware of himself as God, he checked himself for a sudden urge to shout about it, and contented himself with the unconfrontable.

Three hundred more years passed by in the twinkling of an eye. He interrupted his *Time To Himself* and invited an appearance by Mn. This was not to be however, as Mn was pledged to one thousand years of life on earth as an initiate of the fifth order; he was thus able to remain with his body without it decomposing through age. It involved skill, but many have this power and utilise it for the benefit of humanity. Mn was an exceptional student of The New World Teacher, who had now become apparent to a multitude of humanity, although many still treated the idea with suspicion, unaware that what is invited to be by any mind, will in fact be.

Although Gs meditation had lasted some hundreds of years, he still found the confrontable very unconfrontable, and therefore further deviated from his task, with an increased interest in Ptolemy's predictions. He chuckled when tuning to a human mind, when he discovered that it was consumed itself with similar interests. This mind had recently studied some returned space probes which indicated as many had suspected, that there had been abundant water and life on Mars. This mind believed that re engineering the planetary environments by terraforming could transform the barren world of Mars, making human colonisation possible. *Ptolemy would be pleased,* he thought to himself. But it was Ptolemy's mind to which he was in tune, and it reminded him once again that his etheric appearance was similar to his dense body appearance of all those years ago ... *unsightly!*

Ptolemy asked him to leave and this he did for a short while, understanding that this being had moved onwards and upwards, but still found it a strain to communicate telepathically into the etheric world. G decided to contribute some knowledge to this space postulate world he had become a small part of, and once again thought for a number of years. His contemplations were superior to the words which describe them, but alas, these words are the tools we insist upon using for the work of transmitting concepts between consenting adults, so we do ... use them that is; until we decide we can utilise something better for which we are already equipped. The latest addition to the human brain is called the neo-cortex, and this enables the telepathic transmission and reception of mind thoughts. Much as an athlete builds his muscle through exercise and good food, so must we feed and nurture this latent power we so often undermine.

As G thought, the following words were his reward, which he passed onto Ptolemy's new incarnation, as a service to humanity ... *time travel is now possible. Faster than light travel, will mean that it is possible to return from a journey younger than when that journey began. Other universes await our graduation, and although more than twenty billion light years away in distance, they know we shall soon meet.*

Then some real inspiration kicked in from a being so far removed from any kind of dense body, whether etheric or otherwise, that it really knocked six hundred years of energy from Gs non-breathing life ... *wormholes formed from gravitational fields, and connecting separate regions of a completely flat universe, will provide high speed travel to these other universes. The challenge will be to enter such a wormhole, as it opens and closes too quickly for even light to pass through. For every fifteen minutes of time which passes on an earth clock, a clock on a spacecraft travelling at the speed of light would gain but one second. It is these space travellers who will return to earth younger than when they left it.*

G was exhausted and Ptolemy delighted, although it had also taken considerable endurance for him to absorb Gs thoughts. It struck G that he could perhaps learn the unconfrontable from his incarnate friend Ptolemy, who was now known by the unfortunate name of Bisley Creeps.

I have done many things in my long life Bisley, began G, but knowing what to do with my life was never as easy as just living it. What is the secret my friend, please tell me as I feel that my etheric years are coming to an end sooner rather than later, with all this absorption of higher cosmic energy which I have been partaking of recently.

Bisley knew all about Gs inability to confront what he thought of as the unconfrontable. He explained thus: *I hinted to you all those years ago what the secret is G, and I knew that it had not dawned on you then, but expected it to have dawned on you by now. Our minds operate on similar frequencies, and during my long period of Devachan bliss in Nirvana, which I decided to use this time in order to gain full strength for Bisley, I understood you to be serving humanity splendidly, and yourself not at all. This goes against you, griffin or not; you must serve yourself AS you serve humanity. But the whole world knows why you could not know yourself deeply enough to perform this self service ... you did not ever spend the time to discover your own story ... you became a part of so many other stories, and please do not misunderstand me G, you performed well!*

I am afraid however, that ignorance is no excuse for serving below par and of this crime you are indeed guilty! Your sentence has already passed however, in living a life beneath that which your karma would have allowed. You are a great being G, and I wish you well ... just sense your story and live it; that's all!

G asked one last question of his breathing friend ... *just before you go Bisley, and I understand that you are busy, how do I live my story once I discover just what that story is?*

The signal grew weaker as Bisley logged off ... *there are no rules G; you gotta rock with it, you gotta roll with it, you gotta take your time!*

AFFIRMATION ... I FACE REALITY

Forty Nine Steps

Your Song

G sensed that he had missed an important part of *the griffin* way, explained to him all those years ago. He decided that if he was able to meditate and receive such incredible inspiration as has already been previously explained, perhaps he would tune into his own akashic records and listen to what he must not have heard.

This he did in one split second and knew what he had not known for many thousands of years. It cannot be put into words out of respect for the griffin method of one to one oral tradition, but it seems that Gs experience may have been enough to instigate reform into the griffin breed's way of life. One wasted life is much wasted opportunity! Suffice to say that G was told to stop thinking and start sensing. This he did and was immediately aware of what he should have been doing with his life. I have not exposed the griffin secret by telling you this much.

From a seven thousand year life, G had but a hundred or so years left and he was faced with a choice. Should he continue his existence much as it had been, or should he begin to live his story. It was a challenge which he confronted well, and the unconfrontable became tame and friendly. He would live his story, he would sing his song, he would help others sing their songs and he would definitely help you sing your song.

It is human to be curious as to what exactly was Gs story, but

201

that is the human way. Although curiosity is also the griffin way, the telling of their personal stories is a series of unfoldments rather than an attempt to convey it all in one fell swoop. You may only respectfully ask *how* he would live his story, and the answer is so simple; he would rock and roll with it, always taking his time to get it just right. It was so uncomplicated! It *is* so easy! He then knew that his story was the greatest story ever told!

AFFIRMATION ... I LOVE THE HUMAN STORY

Reflection

This is for you to perform yourself.

Suffice to say that the corresponding age to the forty ninth step, would allow a person in an esoteric sense, to go and find God; whoever, whatever and wherever. This whole book is such a small slice of inspiration that I feel compelled to implore you to continue your quest for an holistic life by addressing that one fundamental issue which lies at the bottom of every real success story ... the fundamental purpose for living ... the personal story ... may you be yours with love ... forever and ever ...

AFFIRMATIONS

MY ATTENTION IS POWERFUL ... I AM WHERE I SHOULD BE ... I HELP OTHERS WITH THEIR STORIES ... I AM AN IMPORTANT PART OF THE UNIVERSE ... I MAKE MY OWN HEAVEN ... I FACE REALITY ... I LOVE THE HUMAN STORY

AFFIRMATIONS

I KNOW WHO I AM ... I AM ... I LOVE MYSELF ... I AM WEALTHY ... I BELIEVE IN MYSELF ... I LIKE MYSELF ... I AM A MILLIONAIRE

WHATEVER I THINK I AM, I AM ... I CAN CHANGE MY CIRCUMSTANCES ... I SEE ALL AS OPPORTUNITY ... I HAVE A HEALTHY BODY ... I EMANATE GOODWILL ... I AM COMMITTED TO MY EVOLVING REALITY ... I HOLD MY OWN COUNCIL

I AM TOLERANT OF OTHER VIEWPOINTS ... I PLEDGE MYSELF TO MY SUCCESS ... I EXPLORE MY POTENTIAL ... MY AFFIRMATIONS WORK WELL FOR ME ... I KNOW MY STORY ... I CONSIDER ALL VIEWPOINTS ... I USE MY ENERGY WISELY

I ENJOY MY OWN COMPANY ... I BELIEVE IN RIGHTNESS ... I LOVE OTHERS ... I AM A SILENT WORKER ... I ENCOURAGE STORY UNFOLDMENT IN OTHERS ... I BELIEVE IN MY WAY ... I AM PREPARED

WHATEVER I THINK WILL BE ... WILL BE! ... I AM AWARE OF MY BODY'S NEEDS ... I EAT WHAT IS RIGHT FOR ME ... I HAVE A BALANCED OUTLOOK ON DIET ... I TELL MYSELF GOOD NEWS ... I BALANCE MY INs AND OUTs ... I AM ME

I QUESTION MYSELF ... I WRITE MY OWN STORY BEFORE IT HAPPENS ... I AM CONFIDENT ... I KNOW WHAT I AM WORTH AND I AM WORTHY ... I LIVE WITH INTEGRITY ... I LOVE AND FORGIVE ... MY HAPPINESS WITHIN ENSURES MY HAPPINESS WITHOUT

MY ATTENTION IS POWERFUL ... I AM WHERE I SHOULD BE ... I HELP OTHERS WITH THEIR STORIES ... I AM AN IMPORTANT PART OF THE UNIVERSE ... I MAKE MY OWN HEAVEN ... I FACE REALITY ... I LOVE THE HUMAN STORY

the **PAC**
Mission Statement

Through dissemination of quality spiritual and worldly material, living the talk and enjoying the Path of Transformation, we aim to render whatever assistance is required for The Journey

Ultimate Goal
Premier State

the **PAC** philosophy

The improvement of personal life through positive attitudes, benefits Humanity as a Whole

Visualisation Statement

A large and increasing membership

We aid members' awareness of positive reading, writing and viewing materials

We help the world, with a constant output of positive affirmations from all members

We influence the world for the better in every way possible

We show by example, that the PAC philosophy works

We influence the Media, and World Governments, with our philosophy

We exist wherever there are people who can benefit and prosper from PAC Principles

We are revered as an organisation of high principle, honour and integrity

We are available for consultation, concerning disagreements between peoples of the world, with the aim of solving all problems on a win for all basis

Happiness during the Return Journey

Phil Murray
Leader of the PAC 4 February 1996

the PAC

Purbeck Mill Lane Felbridge Surrey RH19 2PE
Telephone and Fax 01342 322833

Welcome to the constantly evolving PAC Concept

The Positive Attitude Club accepts applications from anyone wishing to join in with the spirit of the idea. All we ask is that they embrace the philosophy that POSITIVE ATTITUDES are helpful. This is a members' organisation; direction, activities and content ideas are always welcome. In line with our plans for the expansion of this beautifully simple philosophy, every member is invited to begin their own local PAC along the lines of *forward thinking through creative discussion*. In harmony with my own Mission Statement, I shall be available for as many activities as are practical to my own schedule. Large or small, old or young ... all becomes irrelevant when immersed in inspirational interdependence!

Name .... Date of Birth ....:...

Address ....

....

Postcode .... Telephone ....

Occupation ....

Contribution ....
towards seasonal newsletter, meeting costs and general administration

Membership Number .... to be allotted ....

Let's enjoy today, and look forward to a rosy future ... together ...

Phil Murray
Leader of the PAC 4 FEBRUARY 1996

PAC is an acronym for Positive Attitude Club
The PAC philosophy states simply that improvement of personal life through positive
attitudes benefits humanity as a whole
We are a non profit making organisation dedicated to peaceful interdependence
through creative discussion and forward thinking for the world

Suggested Future Reading And Listening

Lord Of The Flies	William Golding
Trouble With Lichen	John Wyndham
The Midwich Cuckoos	John Wyndham
The Chrysalids	John Wyndham
Brave New World	Aldous Huxley
Great Expectations	Charles Dickens
A Day In The Life Of Ivan Denisovitch	Alexander Solzhinitszen
The Book Of Heroic Failures	Stephen Pile
The Return Of Heroic Failures	Stephen Pile
The Richest Man in Babylon	George Classon
The Tao of Pooh	Benjamin Hoff
The Secret Science Behind Miracles	Max Freedom Long
Animal Farm	George Orwell
1984	George Orwell
Candide	Voltaire
Jonathan Livingston Seagull	Richard Bach
How To Meditate	Lawrence Leshan
The Power of Myth	*book and video* Joseph Campbell
You Can Always Get What You Want	*book, single and multiple cassettes* Phil Murray
Before the Beginning is a thought	*book and cassette* Phil Murray
Empowerment	*book, single and multiple cassettes* Phil Murray
The 49 Steps	*single and multiple cassettes* Phil Murray
As A Man Thinketh	*book and cassette* James Allen
Memories	*cassette* Nico Thelman
The Plan	*cassette* Nico Thelman
Doorways	*cassette* Nico Thelman
Your Back	*cassette* Jean Luc Lafitte